I0474593

# ANATOMICAL DIAGRAMS
# FOR ART STUDENTS

JAMES M. DUNLOP

DOVER PUBLICATIONS, INC.
Mineola, New York

## To

THE CHAIRMAN AND GOVERNORS OF THE

GLASGOW SCHOOL OF ART,

IN WHOSE SCHOOL I HAVE BEEN LECTURER

ON ARTISTIC ANATOMY

FOR A NUMBER OF YEARS;

TO THE HEADMASTER MR. FRANCIS H. NEWBERY,

AND TO THE STUDENTS,

THIS BOOK IS RESPECTFULLY DEDICATED

BY THEIR OBEDIENT SERVANT,

JAMES M. DUNLOP.

GLASGOW, 1899

*Bibliographical Note*

This Dover edition, first published in 2007, is an unabridged republication of the revised second edition of *Anatomical Diagrams for the Use of Art Students,* by James M. Dunlop, originally published by George Bell and Sons, London, in 1904.

The plates, which appear in color in the original edition, have been reproduced in black and white for the Dover edition.

*Library of Congress Cataloging-in-Publication Data*

Dunlop, James M.
    Anatomical diagrams for art students / James M. Dunlop.
       p. cm.
    "This Dover edition, first published in 2007, is an unabridged republication of the revised second edition of Anatomical diagrams for the use of art students, by James M. Dunlop, originally published by George Bell and Sons, London, in 1904. The plates, which appear in color in the original edition, have been reproduced in black and white for the Dover edition."
    ISBN-13: 978-0-486-45775-8 (pbk.)
    ISBN-10: 0-486-45775-3 (pbk.)
    1. Anatomy, Artistic. I. Dunlop, James M., Anatomical diagrams for the use of art students. II. Title.

NC760.D85 2007
743.4'9—dc22

           2006102439

www.doverpublications.com

# PREFACE.

SCIENCE AND ART are indeed sisters, but they are very different in their tastes, and it is no easy task to cultivate with advantage the favour of both. Artistic Anatomy is in its nature a scientific pursuit, dealing partly in explicit observation of details of form, partly in the explanation of the causes producing them; while the details themselves are among those with which the followers of Art require to be familiar; and are sometimes of little apparent scientific importance save from an artistic point of view. In these circumstances it is little to be wondered at that this department of knowledge has not been more fully explored.

Properly conceived of, Artistic Anatomy undertakes the systematic study of the particulars of superficial form, the accurate description of them one by one, and the investigation of the structural and functional causes on which they depend.

Among the phenomena to be considered, the proportions of the great divisions of the body one to another claim an important place, and have justly received attention from remote times. Rules have been laid down by which an ideal standard has been sought to be fixed, the deviations produced by age and sex being taken into account; and while such standards are more or less artificial, and not to be too slavishly followed to the extent of an unnatural uniformity, they certainly are invaluable as expressing a mean which cannot be deviated from to more than a limited extent without transgressing the laws of nature and producing deformity.

Each part of the body has also its particular proportions, and the study of proportions passes gradually into that of details of shape. All these details are capable of being taken one by one and systematically described. But this cannot be done either accurately or instructively without reference to the subjacent structures on which they depend, and the actions governing the conditions of such structures.

Subcutaneous prominences of bone afford so many constant points in the surface of the figure, while the softer subcutaneous tissues sometimes occur in masses of such firmness as to be but little affected by change of attitude, and in other instances are flaccid, pendulous, wrinkled or stretched. But the muscles and their tendons produce the greatest variations of local form in different persons and in different attitudes; muscular substance swelling when in action, while tendons are incapable alike of swelling and of altering their total length, but may stand out when they are tightened over the concavity formed by the bending of a joint. Also lines of attachment to subcutaneous bone, themselves incapable of change of form, may in different circumstances be prominent or sunk according to the degree of swelling of the muscles around. Besides all this it must be noted that muscular contractions cause, especially in the face, lines, elevations, and depressions, not corresponding to the shapes of the muscles, but produced by the displacement of skin and subcutaneous fat, as illustrated by the elevation of the cheek and lower eyelid in laughter, and by the formation at the same time of the lines called crows' toes, and it does seem possible that a more careful analysis than has been attempted of the lines and displacements occurring in different expressions might yield better results than are to be obtained from such works as those of Le Brun, Sir Charles Bell, Piderit and Darwin, however valuable these may be. It may also be mentioned that considerations in connection with balance, respiration, mental capacity and race fall within the scope of Artistic Anatomy.

If these views are allowed to be correct, it will be admitted that the field of Artistic Anatomy has never been covered; and if this task be ever undertaken it must be for its own sake, aiming at independent completeness, and not at mere assistance to Artists. Much will thus be brought to light, in all probability now unsuspected, and Art and Philosophy will both be gainers.

While, however, Art is one thing and Artistic Anatomy quite another, and while it is to be acknowledged that beautiful representations may be achieved without any anatomical knowledge, this only shows how much can be done by practised observation led on by intuitive appreciation which, often unconsciously, guides the mind to the accomplishment of its aims. But such success is neither easy nor to be depended on, and the general average thus obtainable cannot be expected to be so good as would be obtained if observation were assisted by acquaintance with the meaning of the shapes observed. The greatest masters, including notably Michelangelo, Leonardo da Vinci and Raphael, have found that to give intelligence to their efforts at representation, and enable them to understand the indispensable relations of parts it was necessary to call in the aid of dissection. For the eye, though often, even when well trained, at fault, especially when invention is brought into play, is yet subtle to detect instinctively the unsatisfactoriness of error.

It seems sometimes to be supposed that Artistic Anatomy is merely Anatomy made easy for Artists by omitting explicit details and all mention of internal organs,—superficial Anatomy in both senses of the word. But what is superficial in the sense of being slovenly is of little use to any one. The Professional Anatomist addressing his discourse to Artists, and desiring to give them the information for which they crave, cannot help seeing at once that there is much internal structure which can have no possible bearing on Art, but he will fail altogether in his purpose if he does not note that the artist seeks for direction with regard to details which are often of small interest to the surgeon, and have received little attention from Anatomists.

Two of the sets of considerations most important to the Artist will easily be seen to be, one, the part played by the skeleton in determining the external form, and another, the precise extent and attachments of superficial muscles, together with the disposition of muscular fibre and tendon in individual muscles. It is principally to these two considerations that Mr. Dunlop directs attention in the following pages, appealing to the eye, instead of depending on description ; and it appears to me that the method which he has selected, and the manner in which he has carried it out, provide for the Art Student a singularly compendious and desirable book, easily consulted, and occupying ground which has not hitherto been taken up. It is not the whole subject of Artistic Anatomy, but only one department of it which is here dealt with. The facts taught are brought out with diagrammatic simplicity and precision which cannot fail to bring them clearly and prominently before the student, thus giving him immense assistance. I have pleasure therefore in anticipating for this useful work a great success.

JOHN CLELAND.

# CONTENTS.

CONTENTS.

# ANATOMICAL DIAGRAMS FOR ART STUDENTS

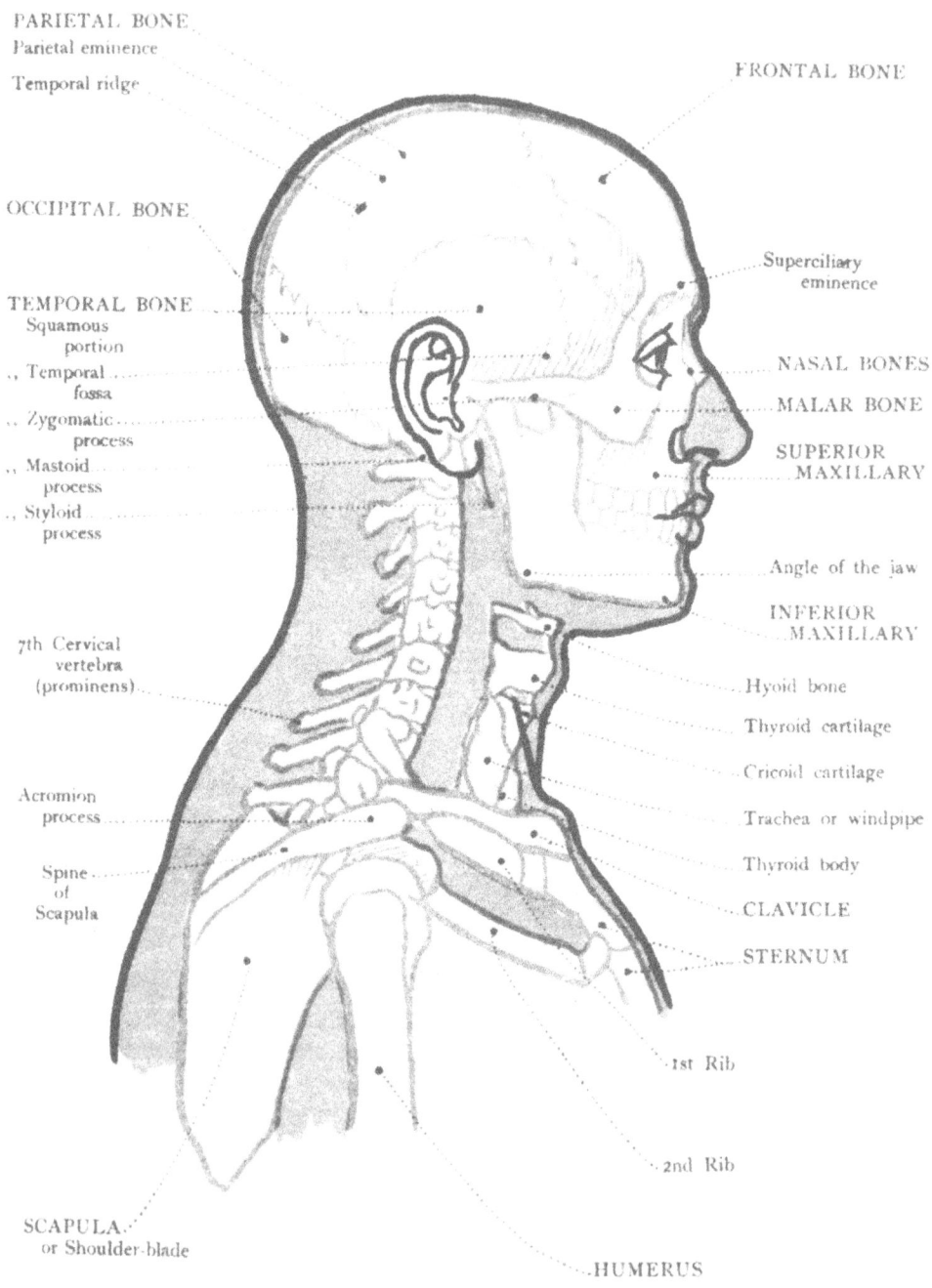

PARIETAL BONE
Parietal eminence

Temporal ridge

FRONTAL BONE

OCCIPITAL BONE

Superciliary
eminence

TEMPORAL BONE
Squamous
portion
., Temporal
fossa

NASAL BONES

.. Zygomatic
process

MALAR BONE

SUPERIOR
MAXILLARY

., Mastoid
process

.. Styloid
process

Angle of the jaw

INFERIOR
MAXILLARY

7th Cervical
vertebra
(prominens)

Hyoid bone

Thyroid cartilage

Cricoid cartilage

Acromion
process

Trachea or windpipe

Spine
of
Scapula

Thyroid body

CLAVICLE

STERNUM

1st Rib

2nd Rib

SCAPULA
or Shoulder-blade

HUMERUS

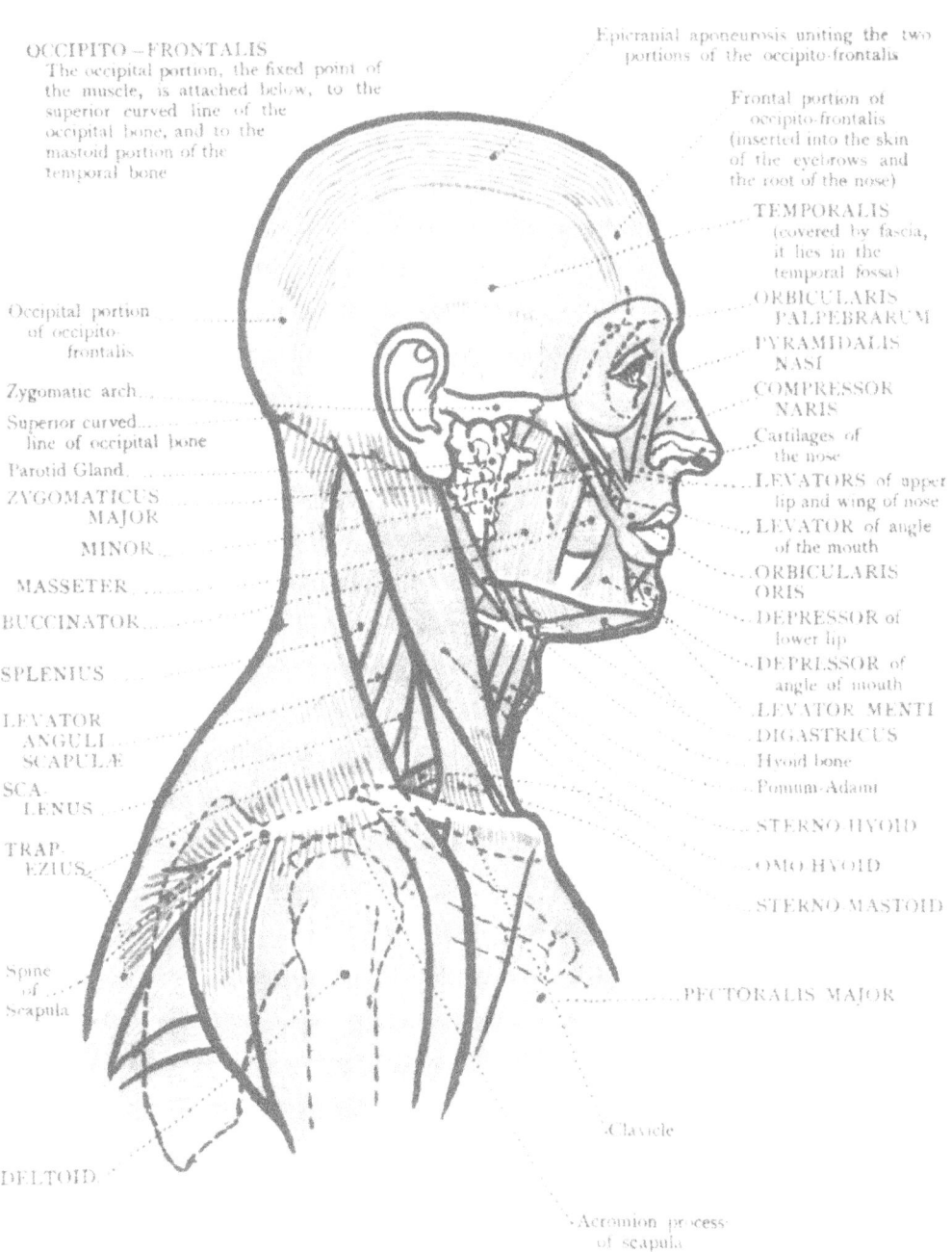

OCCIPITO—FRONTALIS
The occipital portion, the fixed point of
the muscle, is attached below, to the
superior curved line of the
occipital bone, and to the
mastoid portion of the
temporal bone

Occipital portion
of occipito-
frontalis

Zygomatic arch

Superior curved
line of occipital bone

Parotid Gland

ZYGOMATICUS
MAJOR

MINOR

MASSETER

BUCCINATOR

SPLENIUS

LEVATOR
ANGULI
SCAPULÆ

SCA-
LENUS

TRAP-
EZIUS

Spine
of
Scapula

DELTOID

Epicranial aponeurosis uniting the two
portions of the occipito-frontalis

Frontal portion of
occipito-frontalis
(inserted into the skin
of the eyebrows and
the root of the nose)

TEMPORALIS
(covered by fascia,
it lies in the
temporal fossa)

ORBICULARIS
PALPEBRARUM

PYRAMIDALIS
NASI

COMPRESSOR
NARIS

Cartilages of
the nose

LEVATORS of upper
lip and wing of nose

LEVATOR of angle
of the mouth

ORBICULARIS
ORIS

DEPRESSOR of
lower lip

DEPRESSOR of
angle of mouth

LEVATOR MENTI

DIGASTRICUS

Hyoid bone

Pomum-Adami

STERNO-HYOID

OMO-HYOID

STERNO-MASTOID

PECTORALIS MAJOR

Clavicle

Acromion process
of scapula

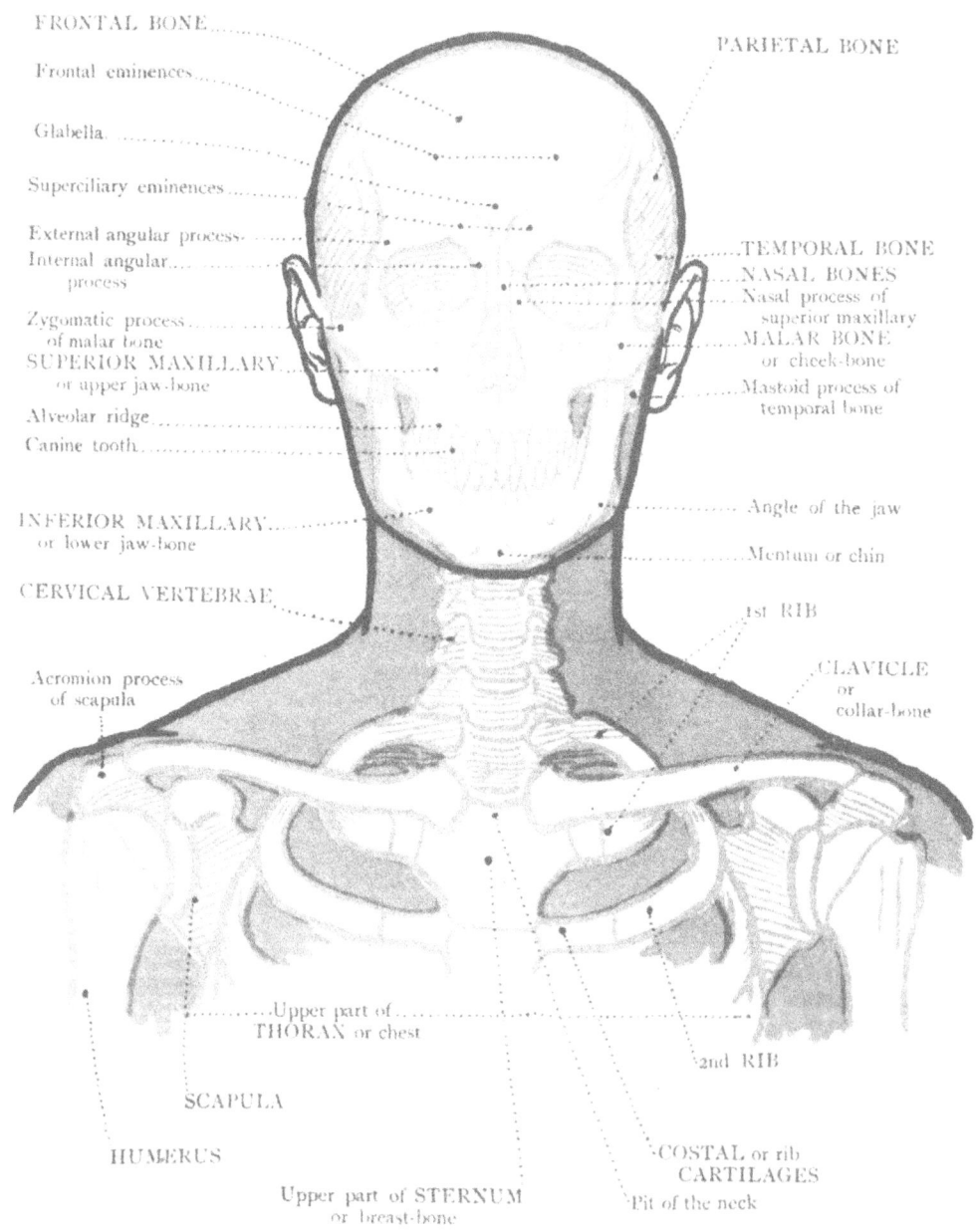

FRONTAL BONE

Frontal eminences

Glabella

Superciliary eminences

External angular process
Internal angular
process

Zygomatic process
of malar bone
SUPERIOR MAXILLARY
or upper jaw-bone

Alveolar ridge

Canine tooth

INFERIOR MAXILLARY
or lower jaw-bone

CERVICAL VERTEBRAE

Acromion process
of scapula

PARIETAL BONE

TEMPORAL BONE
NASAL BONES
Nasal process of
superior maxillary
MALAR BONE
or cheek-bone
Mastoid process of
temporal bone

Angle of the jaw

Mentum or chin

1st RIB

CLAVICLE
or
collar-bone

Upper part of
THORAX or chest

SCAPULA

HUMERUS

Upper part of STERNUM
or breast-bone

2nd RIB

COSTAL or rib
CARTILAGES
Pit of the neck

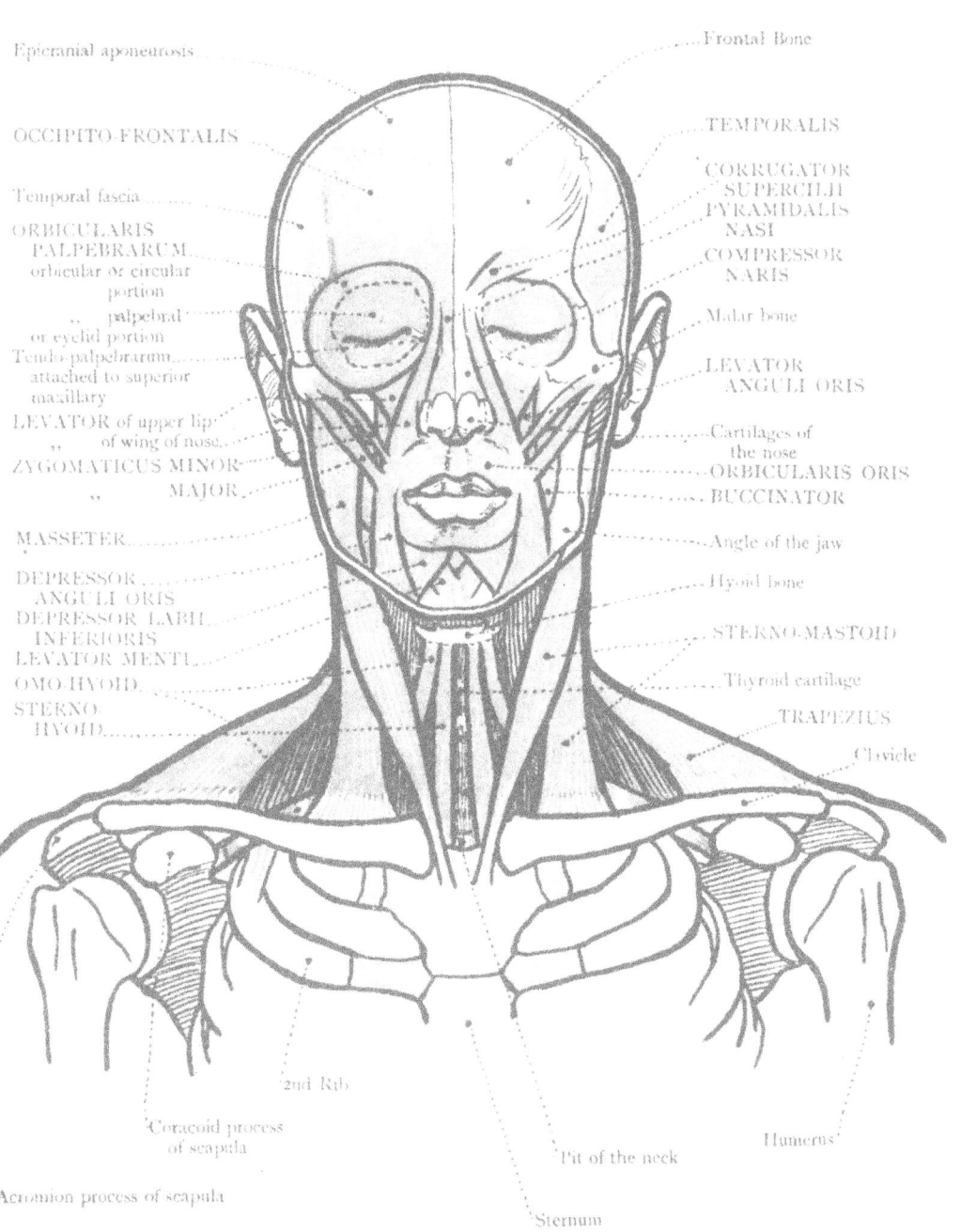

Epicranial aponeurosis

Frontal Bone

OCCIPITO-FRONTALIS

TEMPORALIS

Temporal fascia

CORRUGATOR
SUPERCILII
PYRAMIDALIS
NASI
COMPRESSOR
NARIS

ORBICULARIS
PALPEBRARUM
orbicular or circular
portion
palpebral
or eyelid portion
Tendo-palpebrarum
attached to superior
maxillary

Malar bone

LEVATOR
ANGULI ORIS

LEVATOR of upper lip
,,  of wing of nose
ZYGOMATICUS MINOR
,,  MAJOR

Cartilages of
the nose
ORBICULARIS ORIS
BUCCINATOR

MASSETER

Angle of the jaw

DEPRESSOR
ANGULI ORIS
DEPRESSOR LABII
INFERIORIS
LEVATOR MENTI
OMO-HYOID
STERNO-
HYOID

Hyoid bone

STERNO-MASTOID

Thyroid cartilage

TRAPEZIUS

Clavicle

2nd Rib

Coracoid process
of scapula

Humerus

Pit of the neck

Acromion process of scapula

Sternum

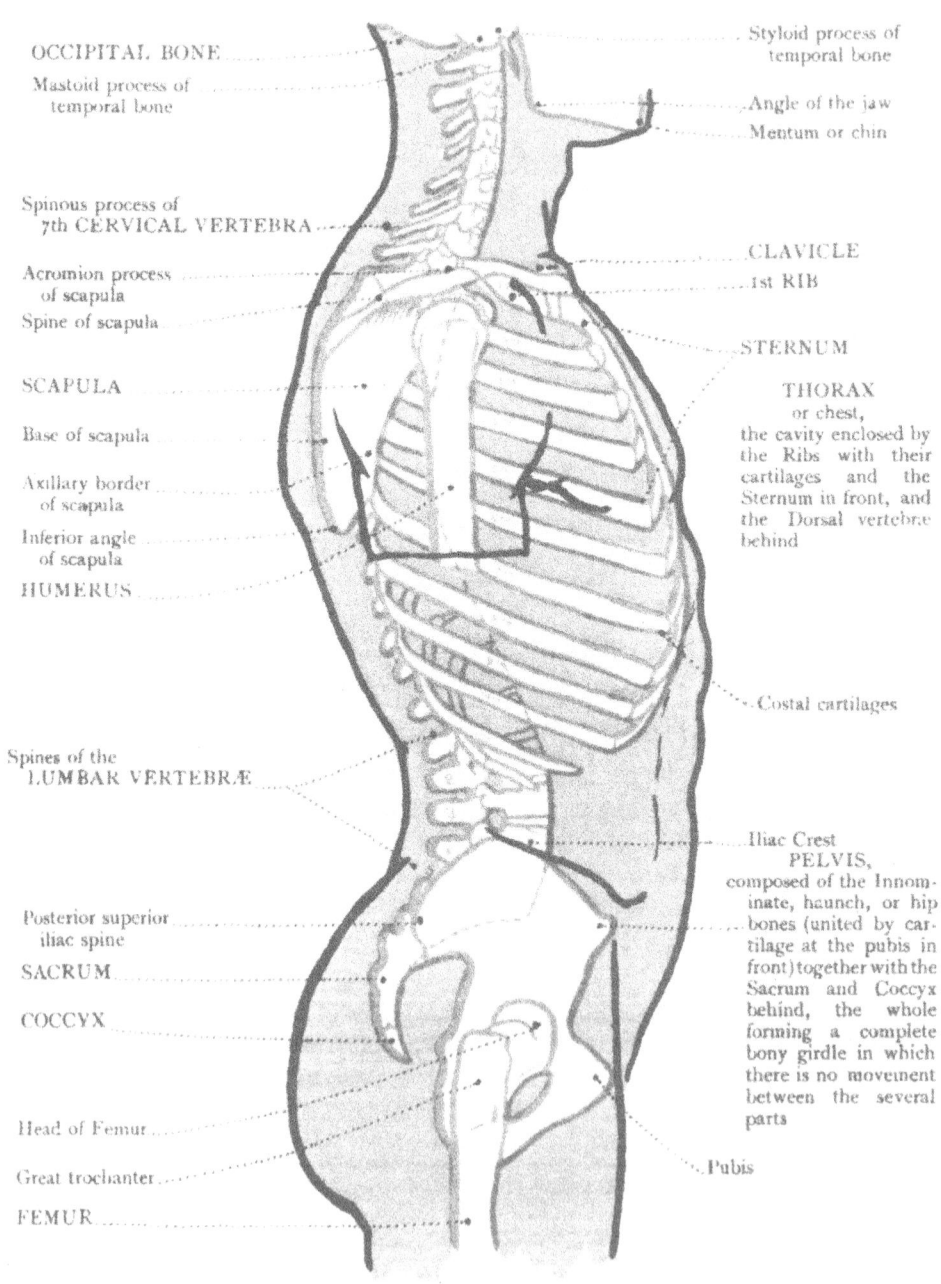

OCCIPITAL BONE

Mastoid process of temporal bone

Spinous process of 7th CERVICAL VERTEBRA

Acromion process of scapula

Spine of scapula

SCAPULA

Base of scapula

Axillary border of scapula

Inferior angle of scapula

HUMERUS

Spines of the LUMBAR VERTEBRÆ

Posterior superior iliac spine

SACRUM

COCCYX

Head of Femur

Great trochanter

FEMUR

Styloid process of temporal bone

Angle of the jaw

Mentum or chin

CLAVICLE

1st RIB

STERNUM

THORAX
or chest,
the cavity enclosed by the Ribs with their cartilages and the Sternum in front, and the Dorsal vertebræ behind

Costal cartilages

Iliac Crest
PELVIS,
composed of the Innominate, haunch, or hip bones (united by cartilage at the pubis in front) together with the Sacrum and Coccyx behind, the whole forming a complete bony girdle in which there is no movement between the several parts

Pubis

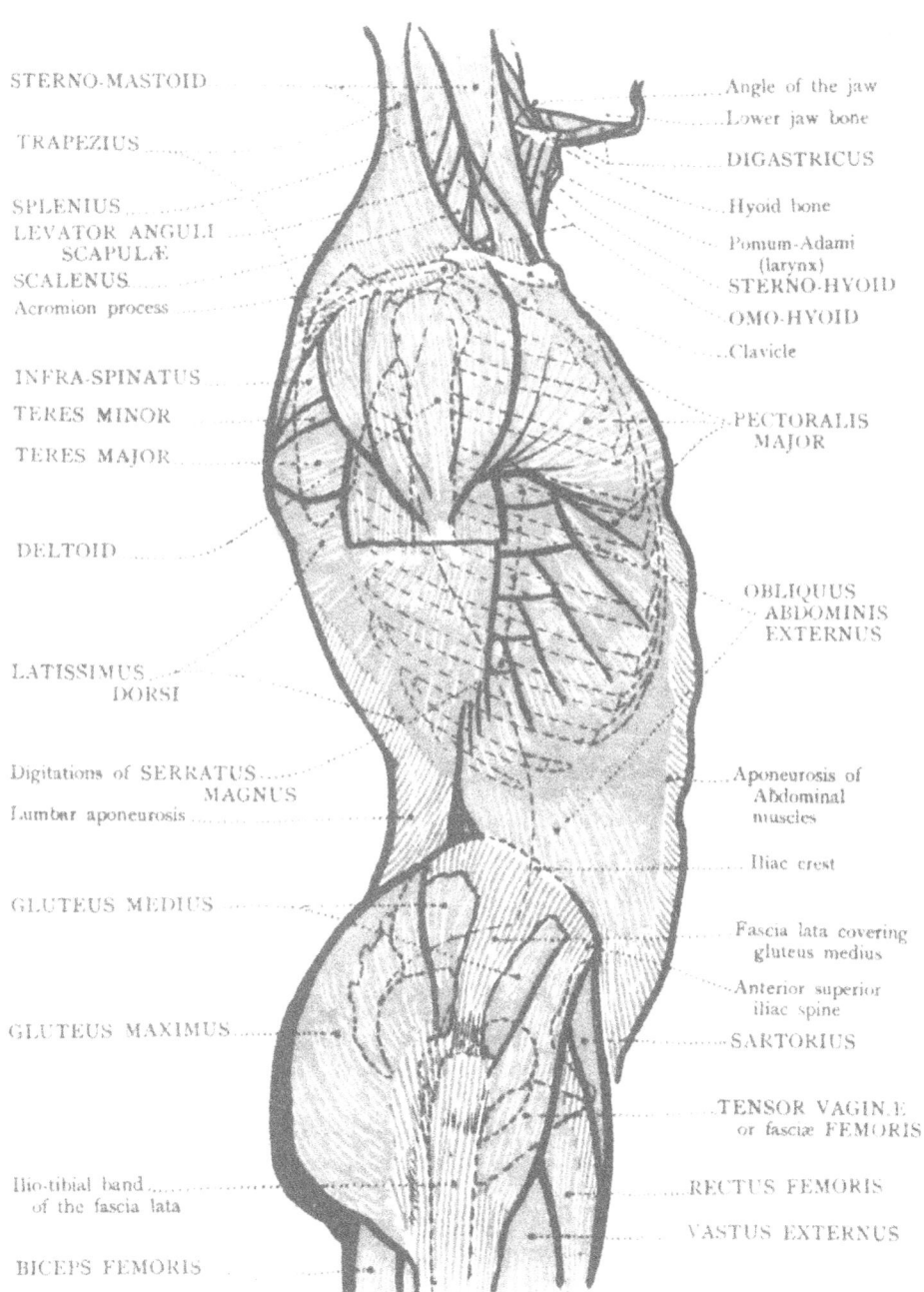

STERNO-MASTOID

TRAPEZIUS

SPLENIUS
LEVATOR ANGULI
SCAPULÆ
SCALENUS
Acromion process

INFRA-SPINATUS
TERES MINOR
TERES MAJOR

DELTOID

LATISSIMUS
DORSI

Digitations of SERRATUS
MAGNUS
Lumbar aponeurosis

GLUTEUS MEDIUS

GLUTEUS MAXIMUS

Ilio-tibial band
of the fascia lata

BICEPS FEMORIS

Angle of the jaw
Lower jaw bone
DIGASTRICUS

Hyoid bone
Pomum-Adami
(larynx)
STERNO-HYOID
OMO-HYOID
Clavicle

PECTORALIS
MAJOR

OBLIQUUS
ABDOMINIS
EXTERNUS

Aponeurosis of
Abdominal
muscles
Iliac crest

Fascia lata covering
gluteus medius
Anterior superior
iliac spine
SARTORIUS

TENSOR VAGINÆ
or fasciæ FEMORIS
RECTUS FEMORIS
VASTUS EXTERNUS

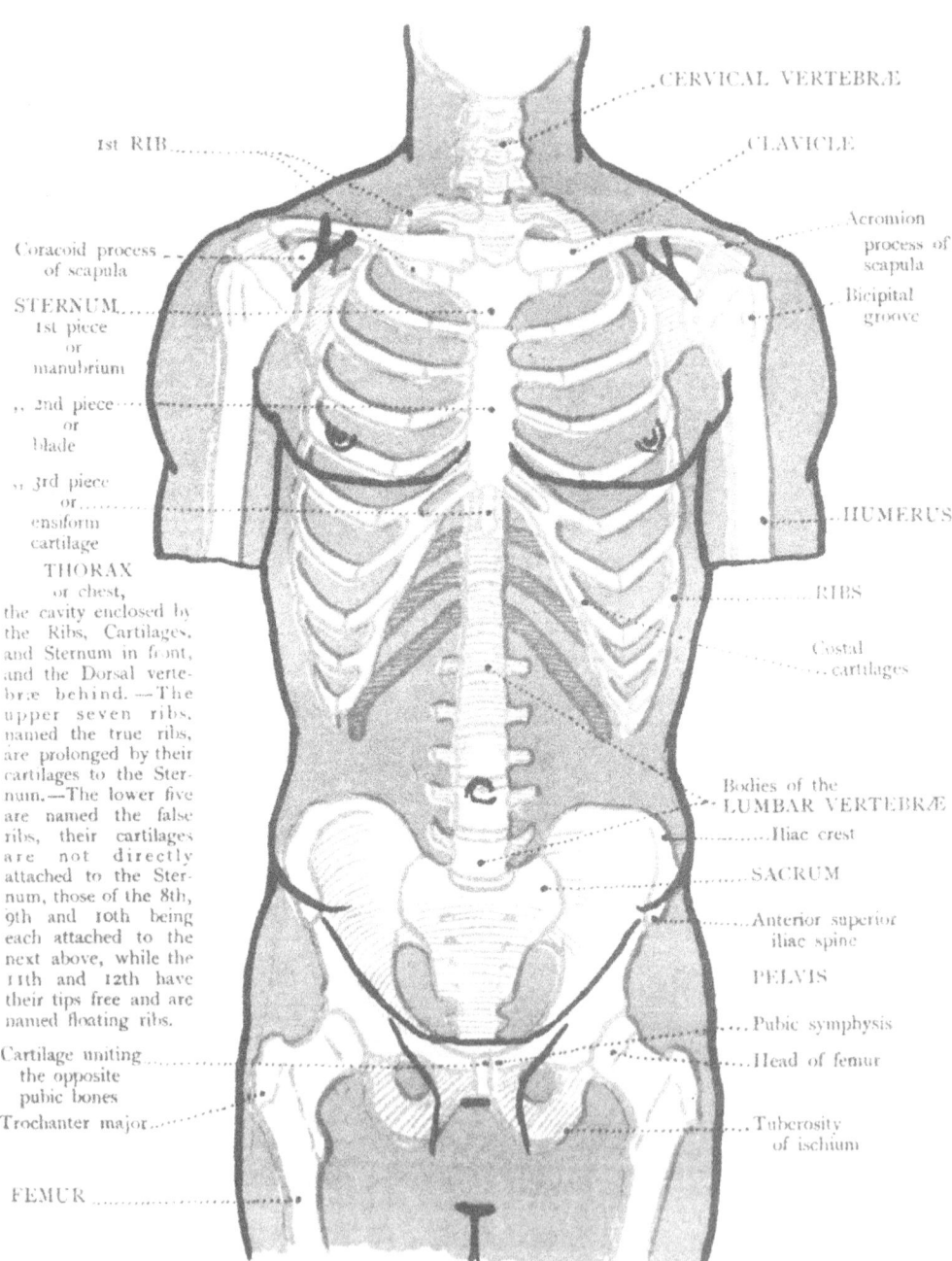

1st RIB

Coracoid process
of scapula

STERNUM
1st piece
or
manubrium

,, 2nd piece
or
blade

,, 3rd piece
or
ensiform
cartilage

THORAX
or chest,
the cavity enclosed by
the Ribs, Cartilages,
and Sternum in front,
and the Dorsal verte-
bræ behind.—The
upper seven ribs,
named the true ribs,
are prolonged by their
cartilages to the Ster-
num.—The lower five
are named the false
ribs, their cartilages
are not directly
attached to the Ster-
num, those of the 8th,
9th and 10th being
each attached to the
next above, while the
11th and 12th have
their tips free and are
named floating ribs.

Cartilage uniting
the opposite
pubic bones

Trochanter major

FEMUR

CERVICAL VERTEBRÆ

CLAVICLE

Acromion
process of
scapula

Bicipital
groove

HUMERUS

RIBS

Costal
cartilages

Bodies of the
LUMBAR VERTEBRÆ

Iliac crest

SACRUM

Anterior superior
iliac spine

PELVIS

Pubic symphysis

Head of femur

Tuberosity
of ischium

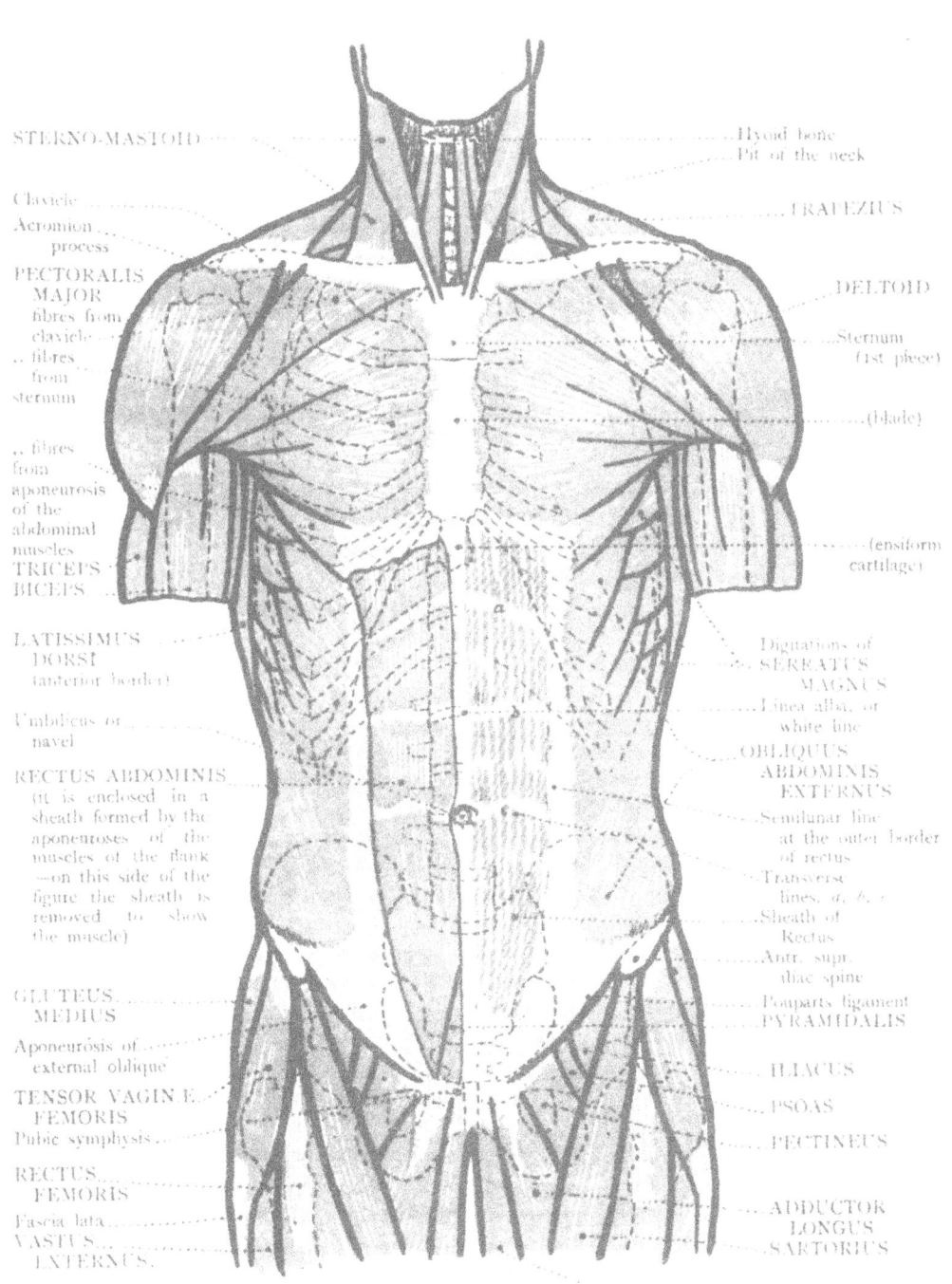

STERNO-MASTOID

Hyoid bone
Pit of the neck

Clavicle
Acromion
process

TRAPEZIUS

PECTORALIS
MAJOR
fibres from
clavicle
.. fibres
from
sternum

DELTOID

Sternum
(1st piece)

(blade)

.. fibres
from
aponeurosis
of the
abdominal
muscles

(ensiform
cartilage)

TRICEPS
BICEPS

LATISSIMUS
DORSI
(anterior border)

Digitations of
SERRATUS
MAGNUS

Linea alba, or
white line

Umbilicus or
navel

OBLIQUUS
ABDOMINIS
EXTERNUS

RECTUS ABDOMINIS
(it is enclosed in a
sheath formed by the
aponeuroses of the
muscles of the flank
—on this side of the
figure the sheath is
removed to show
the muscle)

Semilunar line
at the outer border
of rectus

Transverse
lines, a, b, c

Sheath of
Rectus

Antr. supr.
iliac spine

GLUTEUS
MEDIUS

Pouparts ligament
PYRAMIDALIS

Aponeurosis of
external oblique

ILIACUS

TENSOR VAGIN.E.
FEMORIS
Pubic symphysis

PSOAS

PECTINEUS

RECTUS
FEMORIS

Fascia lata
VASTUS
EXTERNUS.

ADDUCTOR
LONGUS
SARTORIUS

GRACILIS

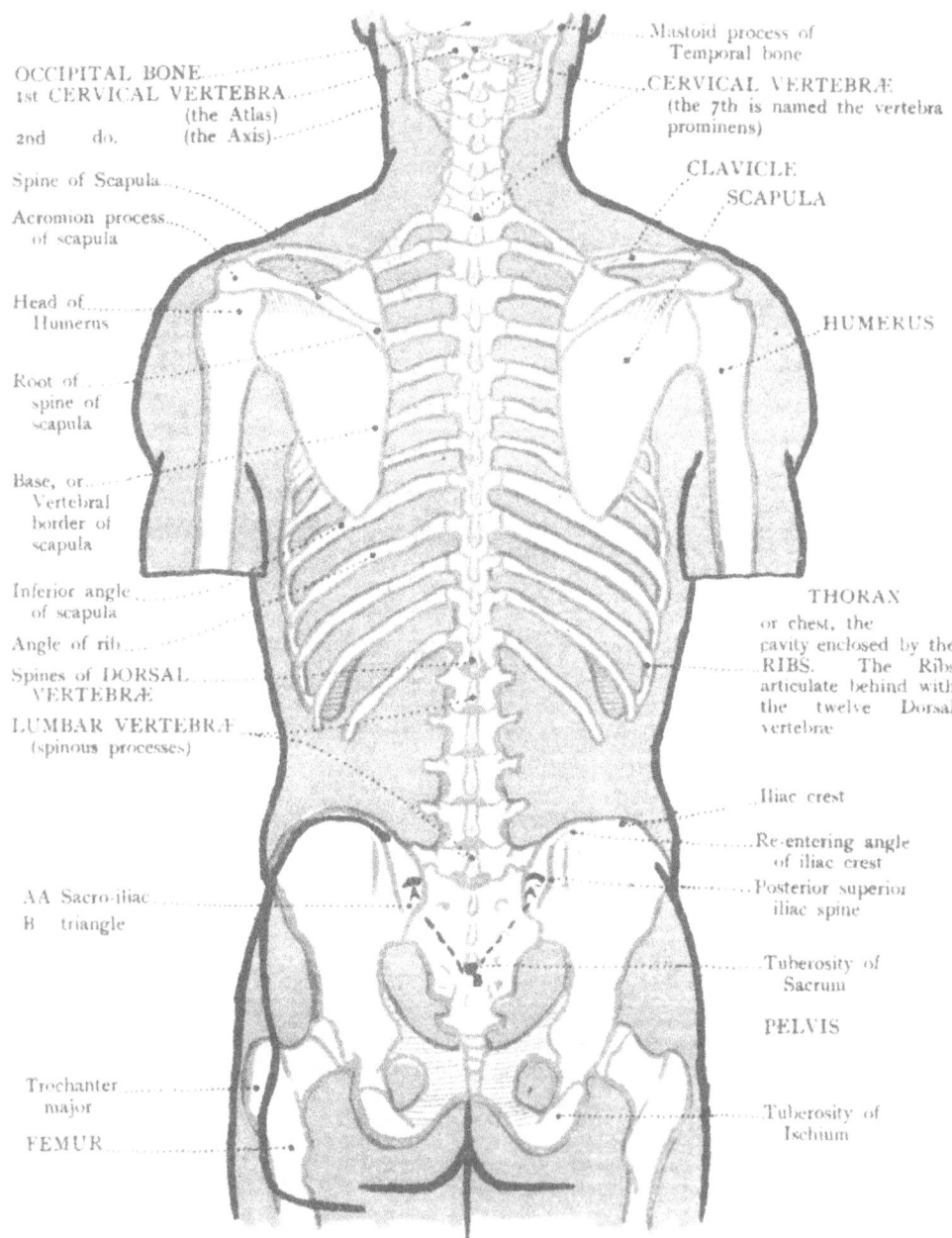

OCCIPITAL BONE
1st CERVICAL VERTEBRA
(the Atlas)
2nd    do.    (the Axis)

Spine of Scapula

Acromion process
of scapula

Head of
Humerus

Root of
spine of
scapula

Base, or
Vertebral
border of
scapula

Inferior angle
of scapula

Angle of rib

Spines of DORSAL
VERTEBRÆ

LUMBAR VERTEBRÆ
(spinous processes)

AA Sacro-iliac
B   triangle

Trochanter
major

FEMUR

Mastoid process of
Temporal bone

CERVICAL VERTEBRÆ
(the 7th is named the vertebra
prominens)

CLAVICLE

SCAPULA

HUMERUS

THORAX
or chest, the
cavity enclosed by the
RIBS.   The   Ribs
articulate behind with
the   twelve   Dorsal
vertebræ

Iliac crest

Re-entering angle
of iliac crest

Posterior superior
iliac spine

Tuberosity of
Sacrum

PELVIS

Tuberosity of
Ischium

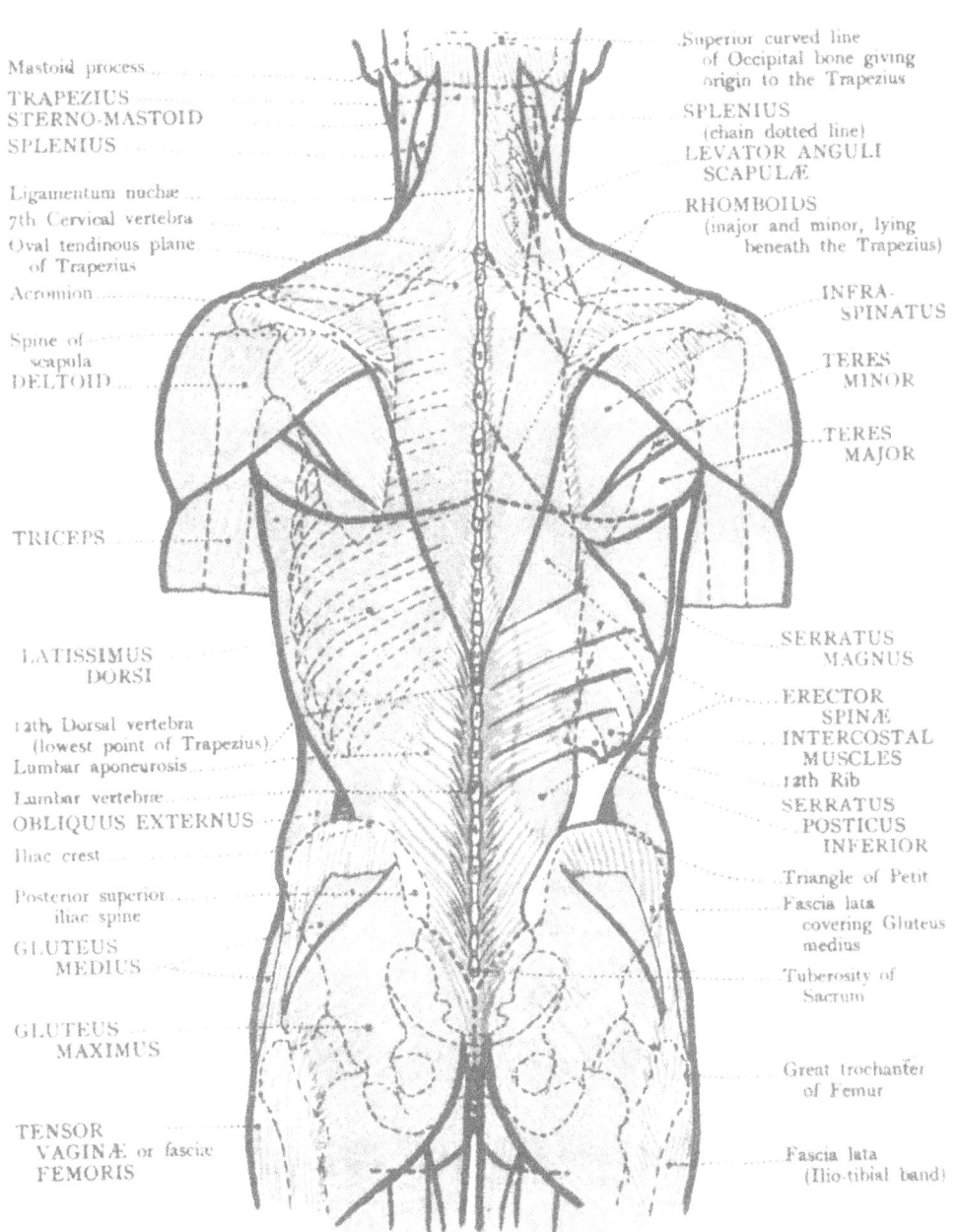

Mastoid process

TRAPEZIUS
STERNO-MASTOID
SPLENIUS

Ligamentum nuchæ
7th Cervical vertebra
Oval tendinous plane
of Trapezius
Acromion

Spine of
scapula
DELTOID

TRICEPS

LATISSIMUS
DORSI

12th Dorsal vertebra
(lowest point of Trapezius)
Lumbar aponeurosis

Lumbar vertebræ
OBLIQUUS EXTERNUS

Iliac crest

Posterior superior
iliac spine
GLUTEUS
MEDIUS

GLUTEUS
MAXIMUS

TENSOR
VAGINÆ or fasciæ
FEMORIS

Superior curved line
of Occipital bone giving
origin to the Trapezius

SPLENIUS
(chain dotted line)
LEVATOR ANGULI
SCAPULÆ

RHOMBOIDS
(major and minor, lying
beneath the Trapezius)

INFRA-
SPINATUS

TERES
MINOR

TERES
MAJOR

SERRATUS
MAGNUS

ERECTOR
SPINÆ
INTERCOSTAL
MUSCLES
12th Rib
SERRATUS
POSTICUS
INFERIOR

Triangle of Petit

Fascia lata
covering Gluteus
medius

Tuberosity of
Sacrum

Great trochanter
of Femur

Fascia lata
(Ilio-tibial band)

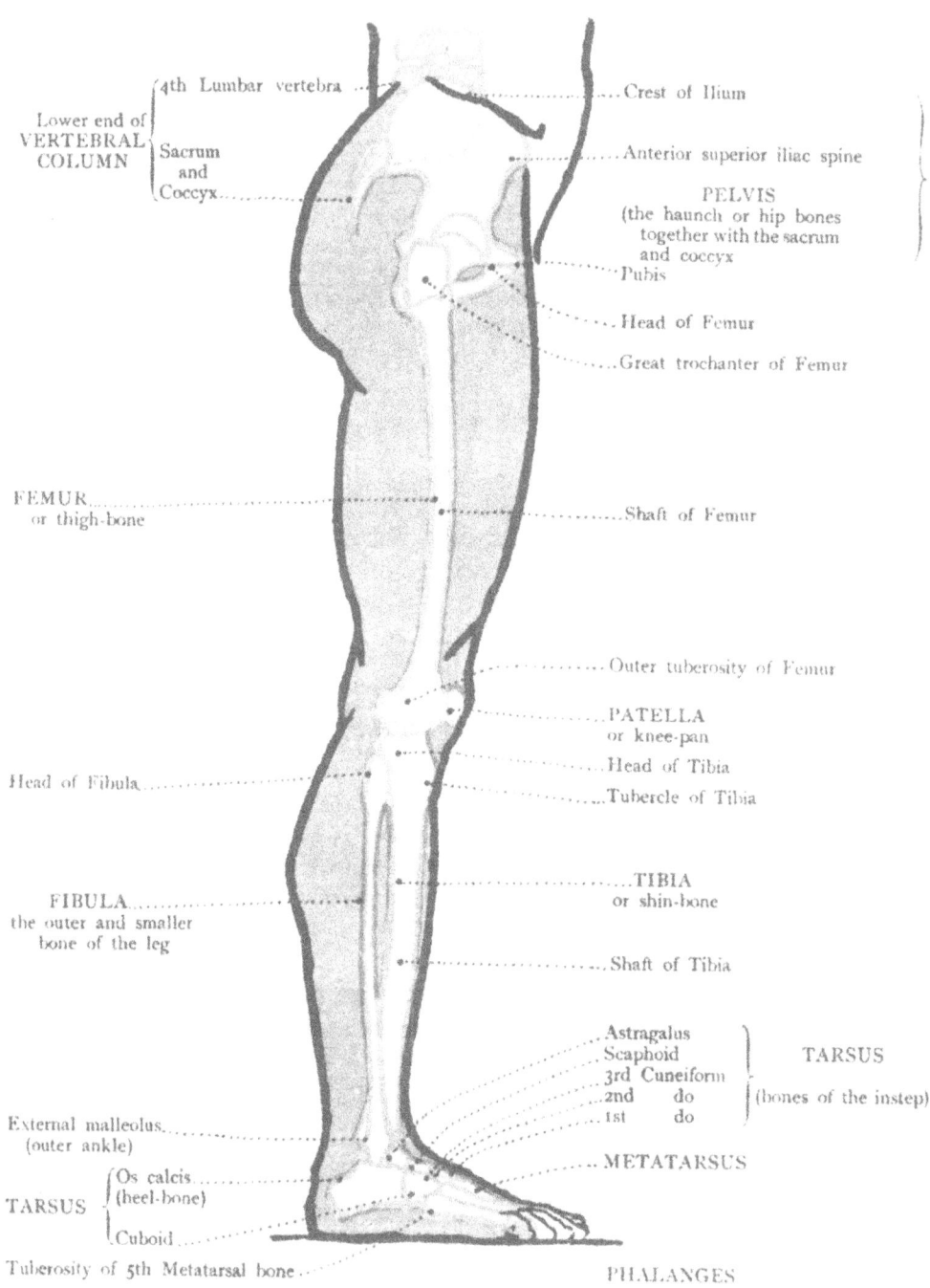

4th Lumbar vertebra ...........

Lower end of
VERTEBRAL
COLUMN

Sacrum
and
Coccyx ...........

Crest of Ilium

Anterior superior iliac spine

PELVIS
(the haunch or hip bones
together with the sacrum
and coccyx)

Pubis

Head of Femur

Great trochanter of Femur

FEMUR
or thigh-bone

Shaft of Femur

Outer tuberosity of Femur

PATELLA
or knee-pan

Head of Tibia

Head of Fibula

Tubercle of Tibia

TIBIA
or shin-bone

FIBULA
the outer and smaller
bone of the leg

Shaft of Tibia

Astragalus
Scaphoid
3rd Cuneiform
2nd    do
1st    do

TARSUS
(bones of the instep)

External malleolus
(outer ankle)

METATARSUS

TARSUS

Os calcis
(heel-bone)

Cuboid

Tuberosity of 5th Metatarsal bone

PHALANGES

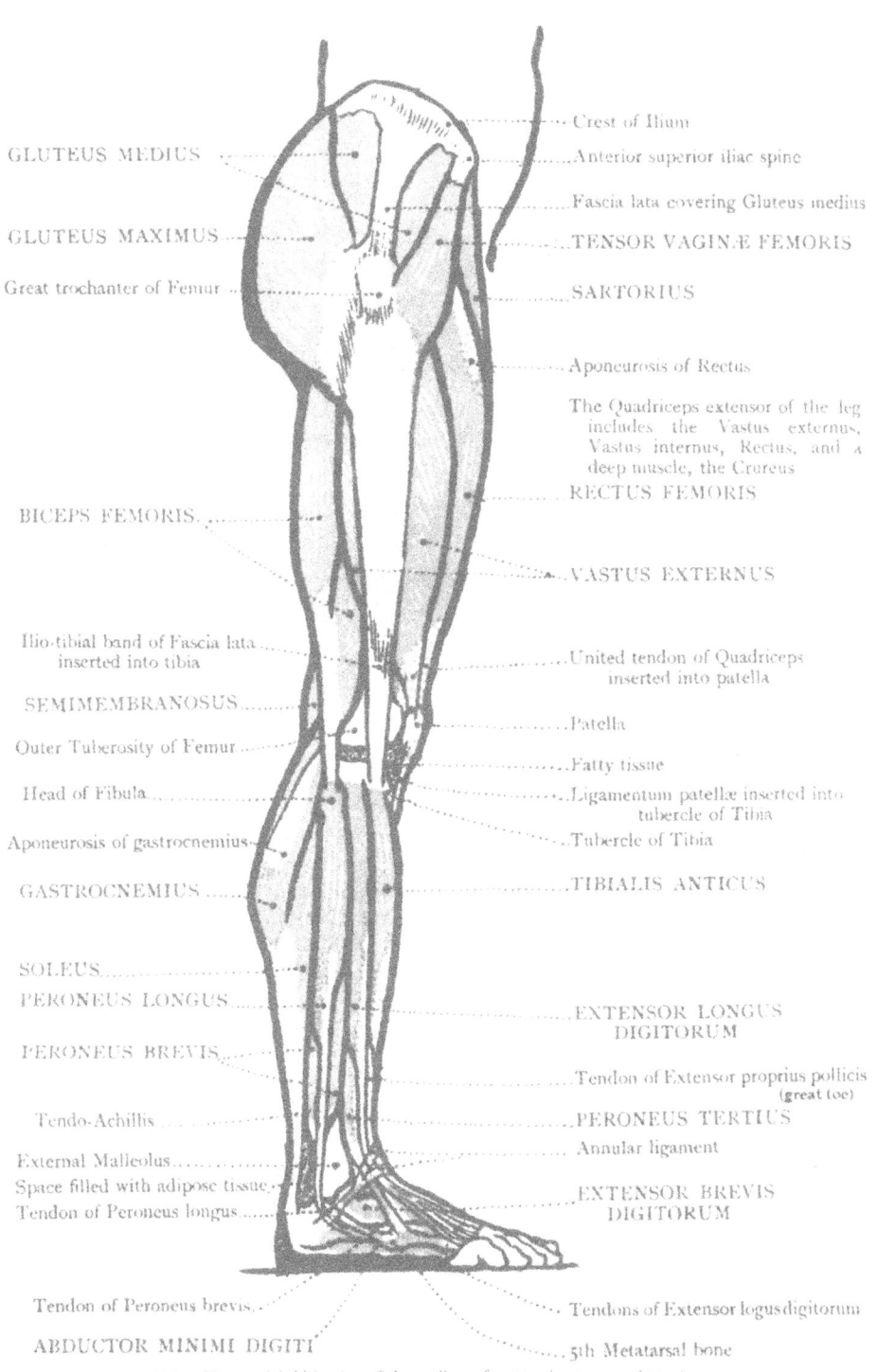

GLUTEUS MEDIUS

GLUTEUS MAXIMUS

Great trochanter of Femur

BICEPS FEMORIS.

Ilio-tibial band of Fascia lata
inserted into tibia

SEMIMEMBRANOSUS

Outer Tuberosity of Femur

Head of Fibula

Aponeurosis of gastrocnemius

GASTROCNEMIUS

SOLEUS

PERONEUS LONGUS

PERONEUS BREVIS

Tendo-Achillis

External Malleolus

Space filled with adipose tissue

Tendon of Peroneus longus

Tendon of Peroneus brevis

ABDUCTOR MINIMI DIGITI

Crest of Ilium

Anterior superior iliac spine

Fascia lata covering Gluteus medius

TENSOR VAGINÆ FEMORIS

SARTORIUS

Aponeurosis of Rectus

The Quadriceps extensor of the leg
includes the Vastus externus,
Vastus internus, Rectus, and a
deep muscle, the Crureus

RECTUS FEMORIS

VASTUS EXTERNUS

United tendon of Quadriceps
inserted into patella

Patella

Fatty tissue

Ligamentum patellæ inserted into
tubercle of Tibia

Tubercle of Tibia

TIBIALIS ANTICUS

EXTENSOR LONGUS
DIGITORUM

Tendon of Extensor proprius pollicis
(great toe)

PERONEUS TERTIUS

Annular ligament

EXTENSOR BREVIS
DIGITORUM

Tendons of Extensor logus digitorum

5th Metatarsal bone

*Note.*—The special thickening of the outline refers to subcutaneous fatty tissue

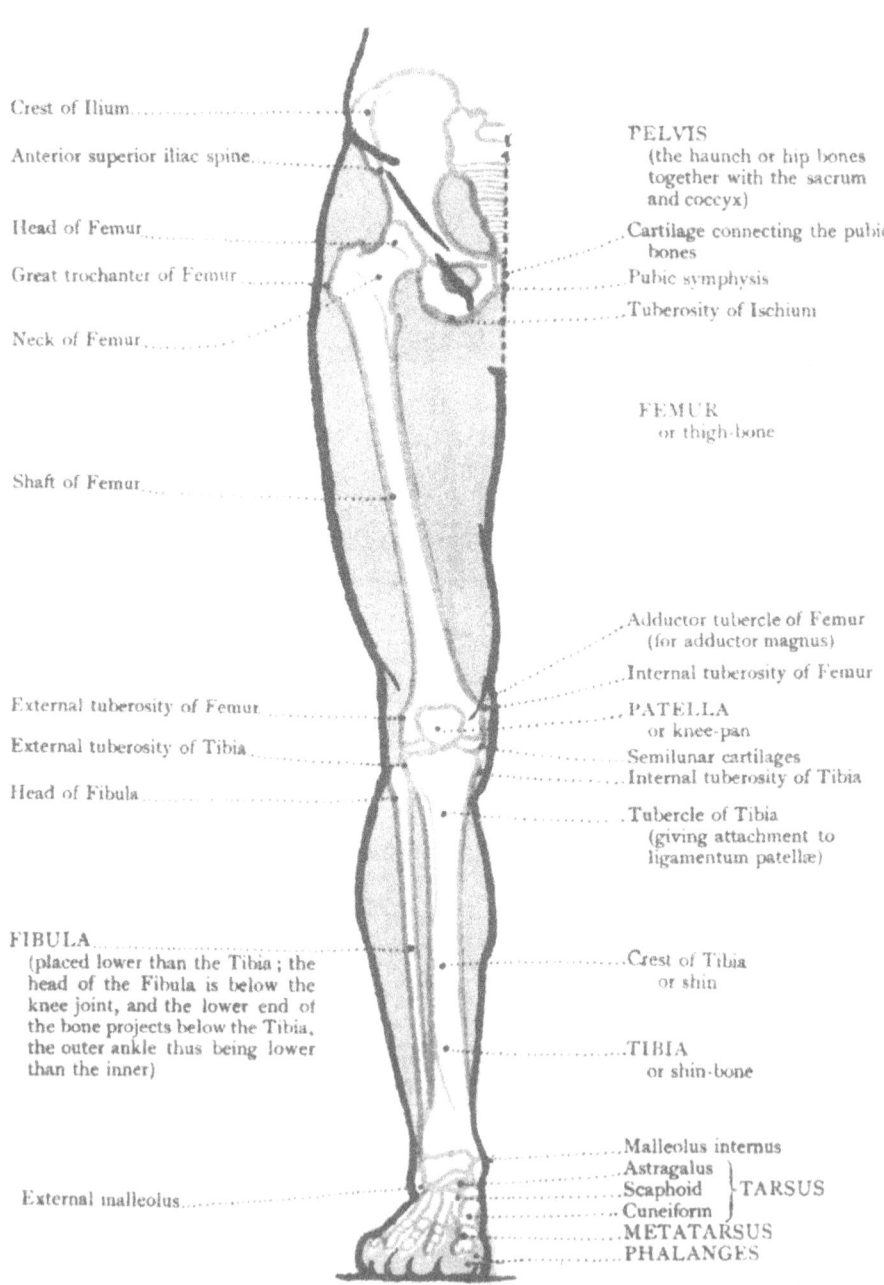

Crest of Ilium

Anterior superior iliac spine

Head of Femur

Great trochanter of Femur

Neck of Femur

Shaft of Femur

External tuberosity of Femur

External tuberosity of Tibia

Head of Fibula

FIBULA
(placed lower than the Tibia; the
head of the Fibula is below the
knee joint, and the lower end of
the bone projects below the Tibia,
the outer ankle thus being lower
than the inner)

External malleolus

PELVIS
(the haunch or hip bones
together with the sacrum
and coccyx)

Cartilage connecting the pubic
bones

Pubic symphysis

Tuberosity of Ischium

FEMUR
or thigh-bone

Adductor tubercle of Femur
(for adductor magnus)

Internal tuberosity of Femur

PATELLA
or knee-pan

Semilunar cartilages

Internal tuberosity of Tibia

Tubercle of Tibia
(giving attachment to
ligamentum patellæ)

Crest of Tibia
or shin

TIBIA
or shin-bone

Malleolus internus

Astragalus

Scaphoid        } TARSUS

Cuneiform

METATARSUS

PHALANGES

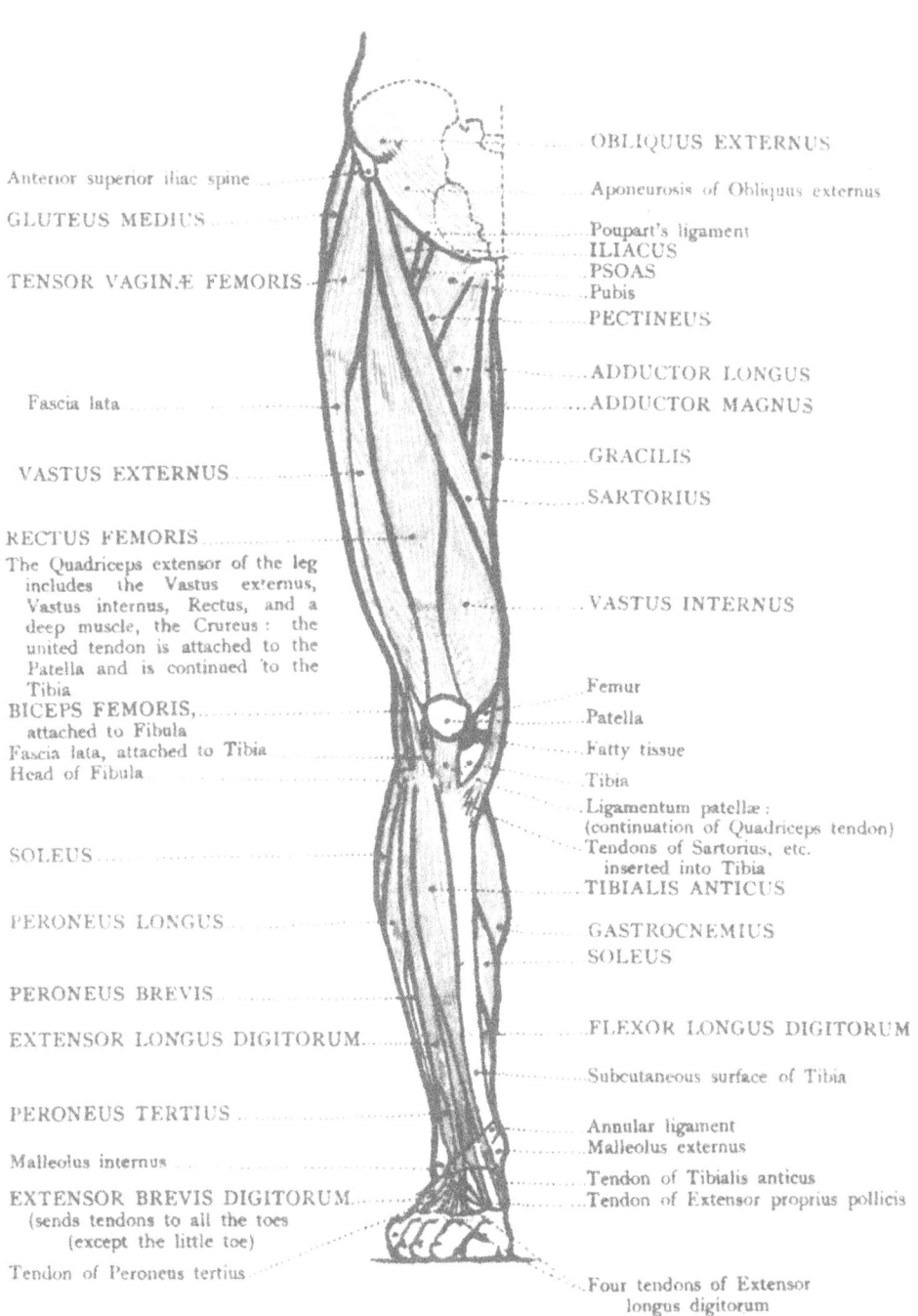

OBLIQUUS EXTERNUS

Anterior superior iliac spine

Aponeurosis of Obliquus externus

GLUTEUS MEDIUS

Poupart's ligament
ILIACUS
PSOAS
Pubis
PECTINEUS

TENSOR VAGINÆ FEMORIS

ADDUCTOR LONGUS
ADDUCTOR MAGNUS

Fascia lata

GRACILIS
SARTORIUS

VASTUS EXTERNUS

RECTUS FEMORIS
The Quadriceps extensor of the leg
  includes the Vastus externus,
  Vastus internus, Rectus, and a
  deep muscle, the Crureus : the
  united tendon is attached to the
  Patella and is continued to the
  Tibia
BICEPS FEMORIS,
  attached to Fibula
Fascia lata, attached to Tibia
Head of Fibula

VASTUS INTERNUS

Femur
Patella
Fatty tissue
Tibia
Ligamentum patellæ :
  (continuation of Quadriceps tendon)
Tendons of Sartorius, etc.
  inserted into Tibia
TIBIALIS ANTICUS

SOLEUS

PERONEUS LONGUS

GASTROCNEMIUS
SOLEUS

PERONEUS BREVIS

EXTENSOR LONGUS DIGITORUM

FLEXOR LONGUS DIGITORUM

Subcutaneous surface of Tibia

PERONEUS TERTIUS

Annular ligament
Malleolus externus

Malleolus internus

Tendon of Tibialis anticus
EXTENSOR BREVIS DIGITORUM
(sends tendons to all the toes
  (except the little toe)

Tendon of Extensor proprius pollicis

Tendon of Peroneus tertius

Four tendons of Extensor
  longus digitorum

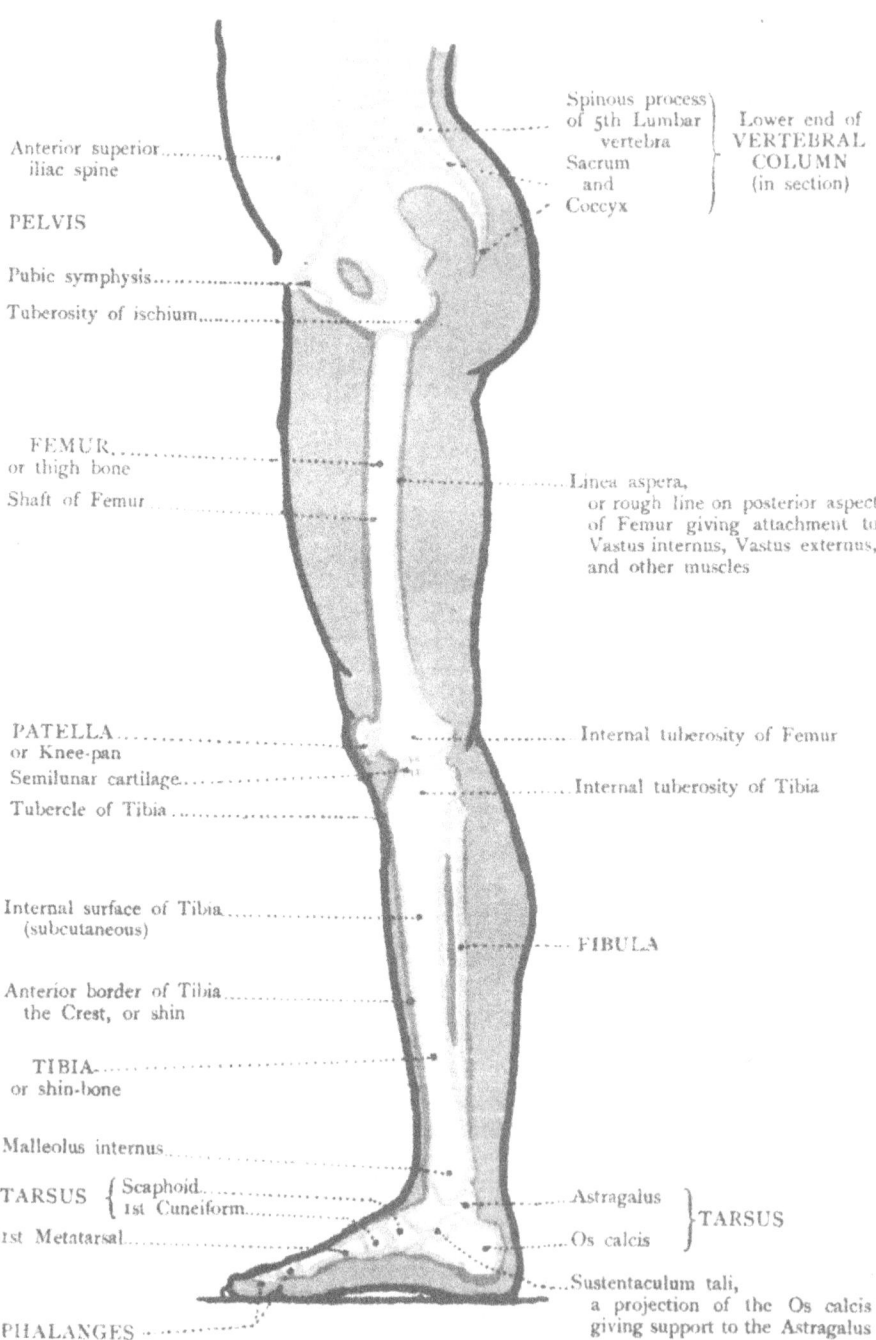

Anterior superior iliac spine

PELVIS

Pubic symphysis

Tuberosity of ischium

FEMUR, or thigh bone

Shaft of Femur

PATELLA or Knee-pan

Semilunar cartilage

Tubercle of Tibia

Internal surface of Tibia (subcutaneous)

Anterior border of Tibia the Crest, or shin

TIBIA or shin-bone

Malleolus internus

TARSUS { Scaphoid
          1st Cuneiform

1st Metatarsal

PHALANGES

Spinous process of 5th Lumbar vertebra
Sacrum and Coccyx

Lower end of VERTEBRAL COLUMN (in section)

Linea aspera, or rough line on posterior aspect of Femur giving attachment to Vastus internus, Vastus externus, and other muscles

Internal tuberosity of Femur

Internal tuberosity of Tibia

FIBULA

Astragalus

Os calcis

} TARSUS

Sustentaculum tali, a projection of the Os calcis giving support to the Astragalus

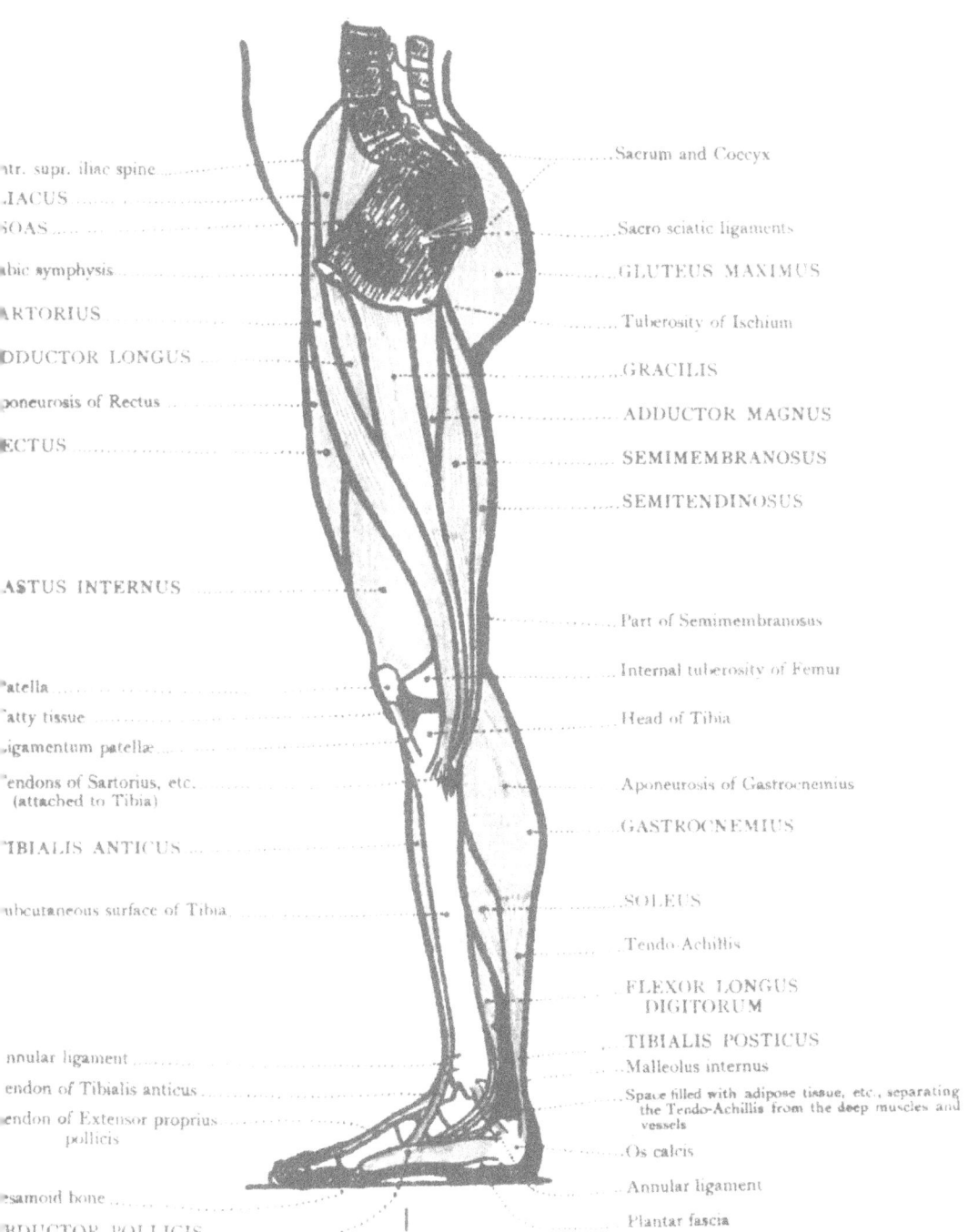

ntr. supr. iliac spine

ILIACUS

SOAS

ubic symphysis

ARTORIUS

DDUCTOR LONGUS

poneurosis of Rectus

ECTUS

ASTUS INTERNUS

Patella

Fatty tissue

Ligamentum patellæ

Tendons of Sartorius, etc.
(attached to Tibia)

TIBIALIS ANTICUS

ubcutaneous surface of Tibia

nnular ligament

endon of Tibialis anticus

endon of Extensor proprius
pollicis

esamoid bone

BDUCTOR POLLICIS

Sacrum and Coccyx

Sacro sciatic ligaments

GLUTEUS MAXIMUS

Tuberosity of Ischium

GRACILIS

ADDUCTOR MAGNUS

SEMIMEMBRANOSUS

SEMITENDINOSUS

Part of Semimembranosus

Internal tuberosity of Femur

Head of Tibia

Aponeurosis of Gastrocnemius

GASTROCNEMIUS

SOLEUS

Tendo-Achillis

FLEXOR LONGUS
DIGITORUM

TIBIALIS POSTICUS

Malleolus internus

Space filled with adipose tissue, etc., separating
the Tendo-Achillis from the deep muscles and
vessels

Os calcis

Annular ligament

Plantar fascia

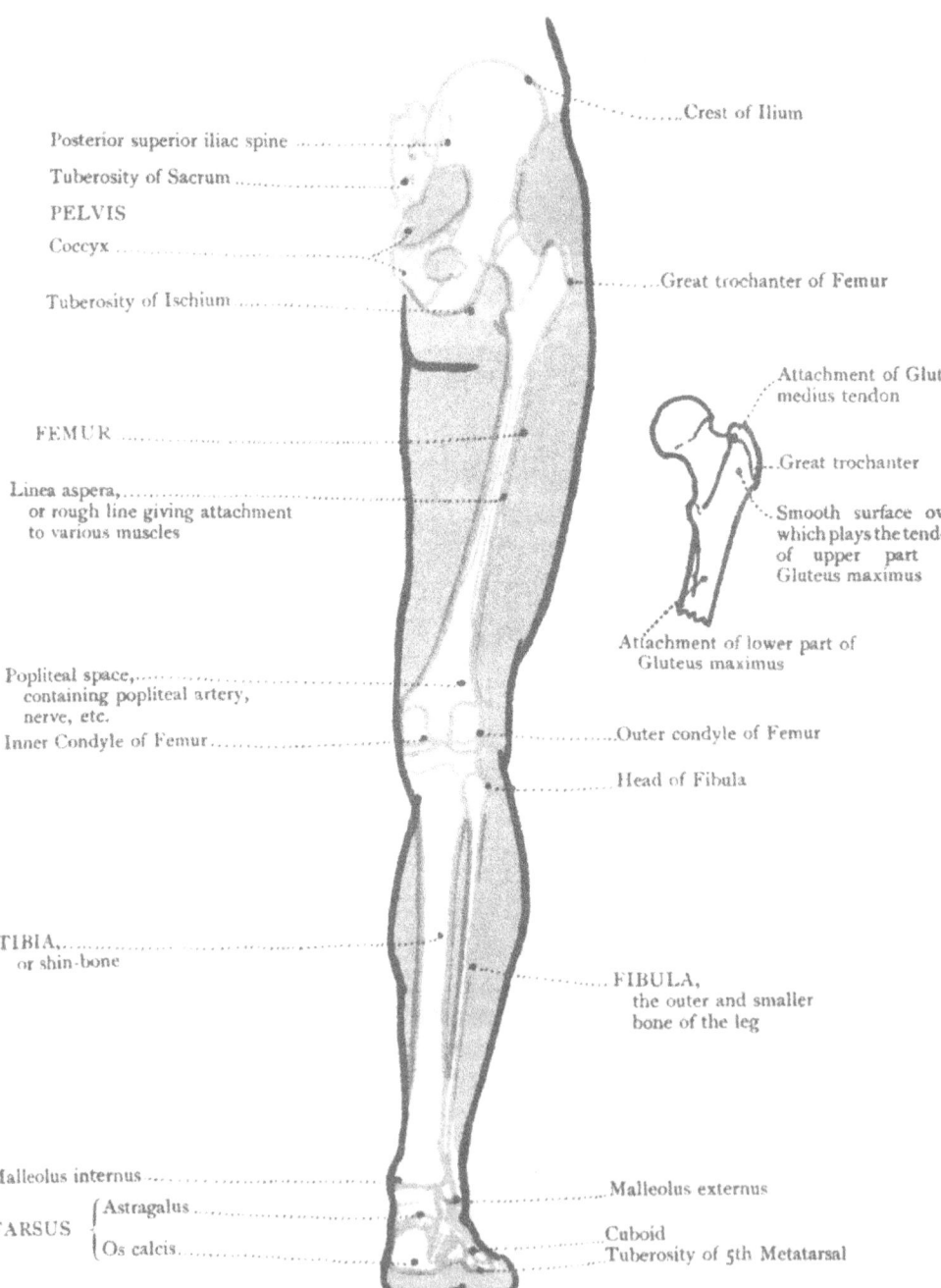

Crest of Ilium

Posterior superior iliac spine

Tuberosity of Sacrum

PELVIS

Coccyx

Tuberosity of Ischium

Great trochanter of Femur

Attachment of Gluteus medius tendon

FEMUR

Great trochanter

Linea aspera,
or rough line giving attachment
to various muscles

Smooth surface over
which plays the tendon
of upper part of
Gluteus maximus

Attachment of lower part of
Gluteus maximus

Popliteal space,
containing popliteal artery,
nerve, etc.

Inner Condyle of Femur

Outer condyle of Femur

Head of Fibula

TIBIA,
or shin-bone

FIBULA,
the outer and smaller
bone of the leg

Malleolus internus

Malleolus externus

TARSUS { Astragalus

Os calcis

Cuboid

Tuberosity of 5th Metatarsal

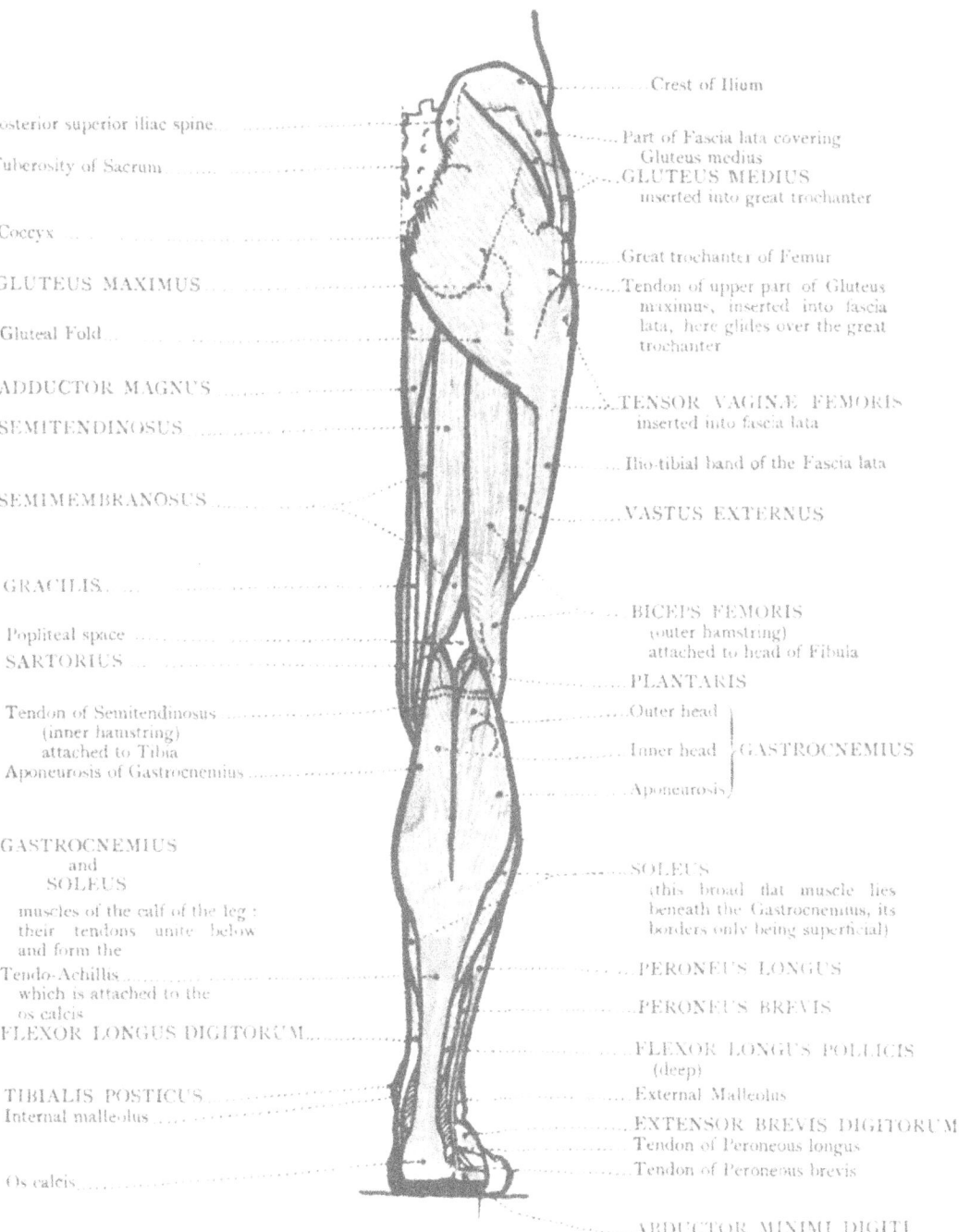

Posterior superior iliac spine

Tuberosity of Sacrum

Coccyx

GLUTEUS MAXIMUS

Gluteal Fold

ADDUCTOR MAGNUS

SEMITENDINOSUS

SEMIMEMBRANOSUS

GRACILIS

Popliteal space

SARTORIUS

Tendon of Semitendinosus
(inner hamstring)
attached to Tibia
Aponeurosis of Gastrocnemius

GASTROCNEMIUS
and
SOLEUS
muscles of the calf of the leg :
their tendons unite below
and form the
Tendo-Achillis
which is attached to the
os calcis
FLEXOR LONGUS DIGITORUM

TIBIALIS POSTICUS
Internal malleolus

Os calcis

Crest of Ilium

Part of Fascia lata covering
Gluteus medius
GLUTEUS MEDIUS
inserted into great trochanter

Great trochanter of Femur
Tendon of upper part of Gluteus
maximus, inserted into fascia
lata, here glides over the great
trochanter

TENSOR VAGINÆ FEMORIS
inserted into fascia lata

Ilio-tibial band of the Fascia lata

VASTUS EXTERNUS

BICEPS FEMORIS
(outer hamstring)
attached to head of Fibula

PLANTARIS

Outer head

Inner head    GASTROCNEMIUS

Aponeurosis

SOLEUS
(this broad flat muscle lies
beneath the Gastrocnemius, its
borders only being superficial)

PERONEUS LONGUS

PERONEUS BREVIS

FLEXOR LONGUS POLLICIS
(deep)

External Malleolus

EXTENSOR BREVIS DIGITORUM
Tendon of Peroneus longus

Tendon of Peroneus brevis

ABDUCTOR MINIMI DIGITI

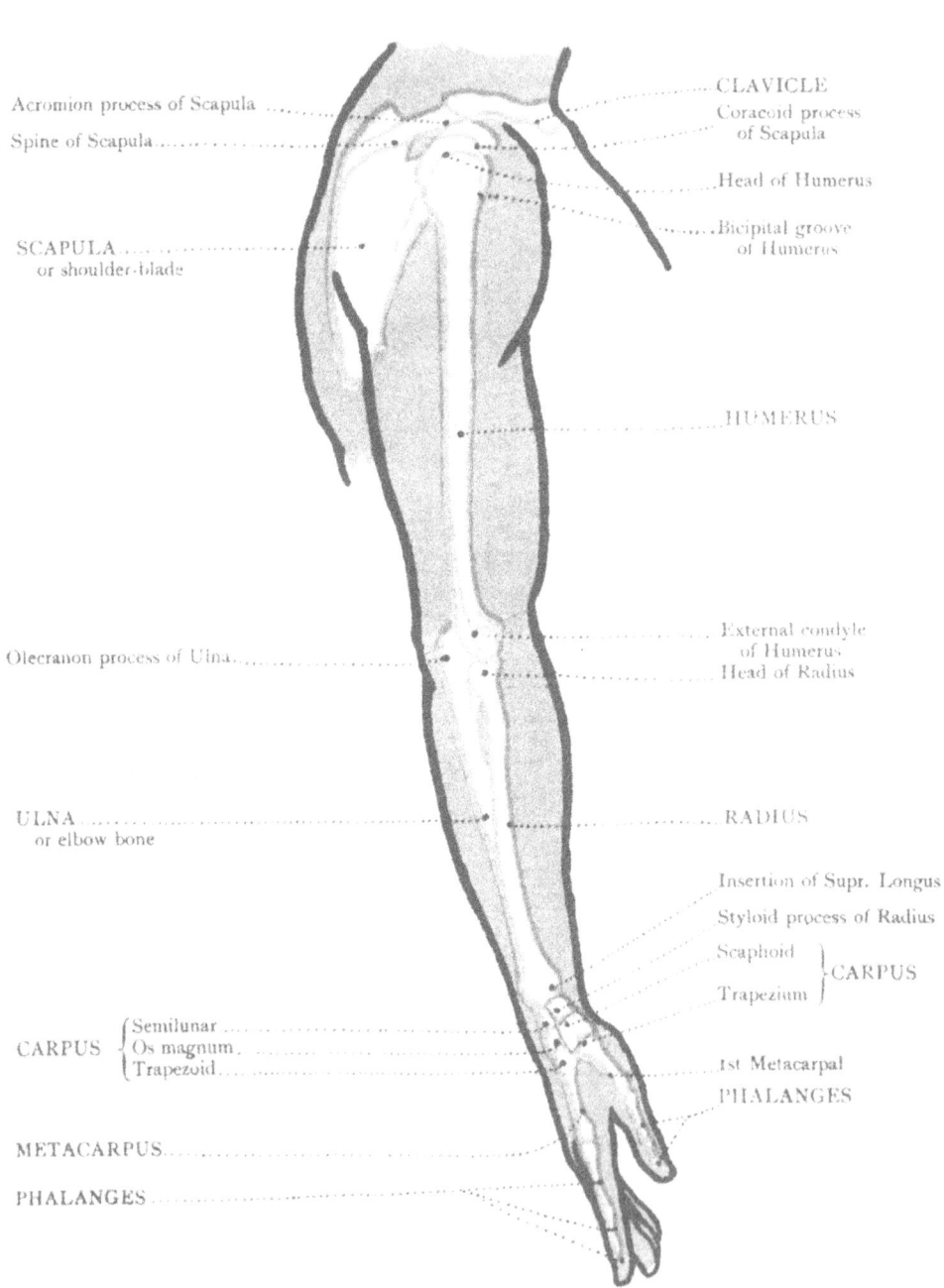

Acromion process of Scapula ............

Spine of Scapula ............

SCAPULA ............
or shoulder-blade

CLAVICLE

Coracoid process
of Scapula

Head of Humerus

Bicipital groove
of Humerus

HUMERUS

Olecranon process of Ulna ............

External condyle
of Humerus
Head of Radius

ULNA ............
or elbow bone

RADIUS

Insertion of Supr. Longus

Styloid process of Radius

Scaphoid
Trapezium ⎫CARPUS

CARPUS ⎰Semilunar ............
⎱Os magnum ............
⎱Trapezoid ............

1st Metacarpal

PHALANGES

METACARPUS ............

PHALANGES ............

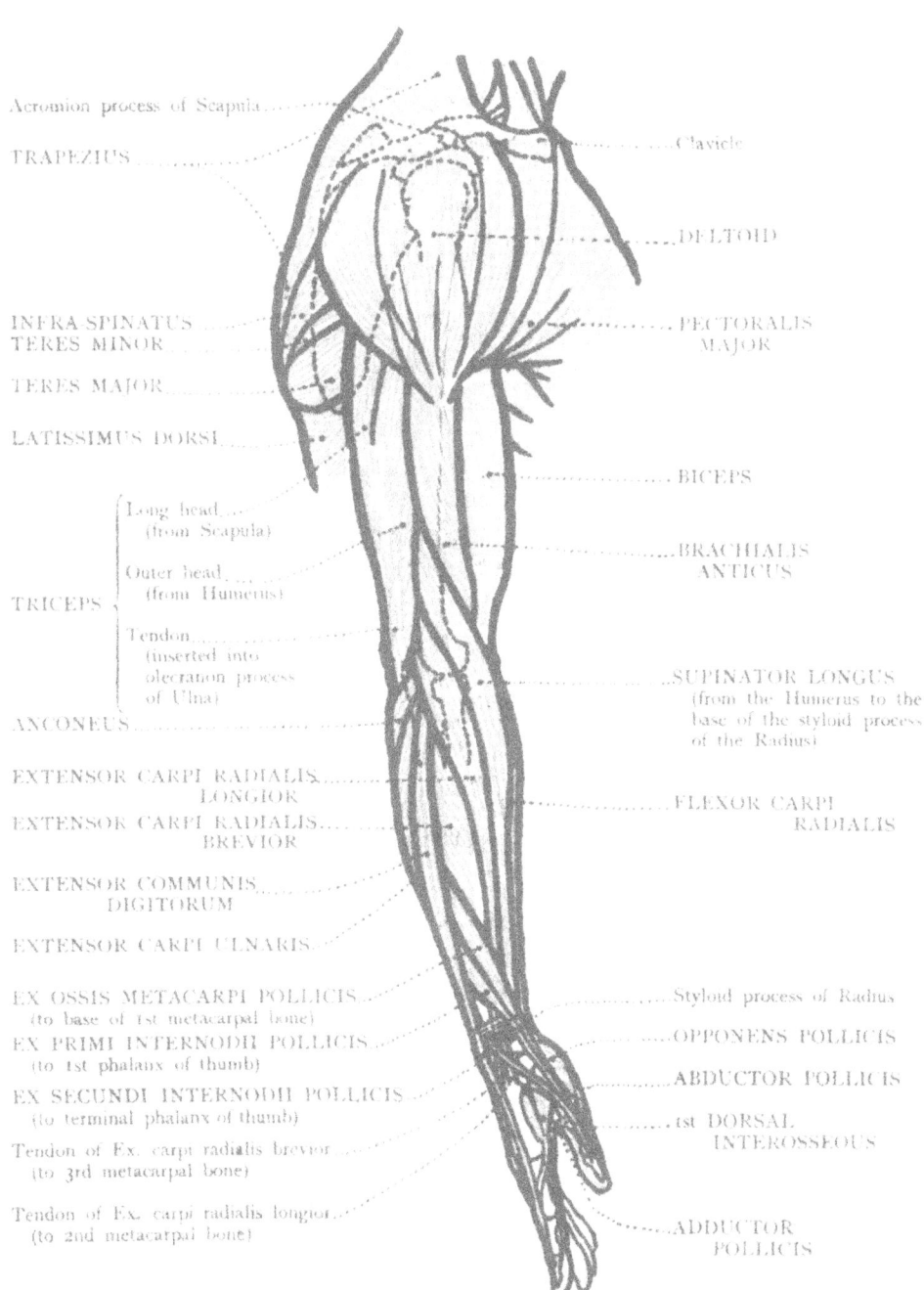

Acromion process of Scapula

TRAPEZIUS

Clavicle

DELTOID

INFRA-SPINATUS
TERES MINOR

PECTORALIS
MAJOR

TERES MAJOR

LATISSIMUS DORSI

BICEPS

Long head
(from Scapula)

BRACHIALIS
ANTICUS

Outer head
(from Humerus)

TRICEPS

Tendon
(inserted into
olecranon process
of Ulna)

SUPINATOR LONGUS
(from the Humerus to the
base of the styloid process
of the Radus)

ANCONEUS

EXTENSOR CARPI RADIALIS
LONGIOR

FLEXOR CARPI
RADIALIS

EXTENSOR CARPI RADIALIS
BREVIOR

EXTENSOR COMMUNIS
DIGITORUM

EXTENSOR CARPI ULNARIS

EX OSSIS METACARPI POLLICIS
(to base of 1st metacarpal bone)

Styloid process of Radius

OPPONENS POLLICIS

EX PRIMI INTERNODII POLLICIS
(to 1st phalanx of thumb)

ABDUCTOR POLLICIS

EX SECUNDI INTERNODII POLLICIS
(to terminal phalanx of thumb)

1st DORSAL
INTEROSSEOUS

Tendon of Ex. carpi radialis brevior
(to 3rd metacarpal bone)

Tendon of Ex. carpi radialis longior
(to 2nd metacarpal bone)

ADDUCTOR
POLLICIS

21

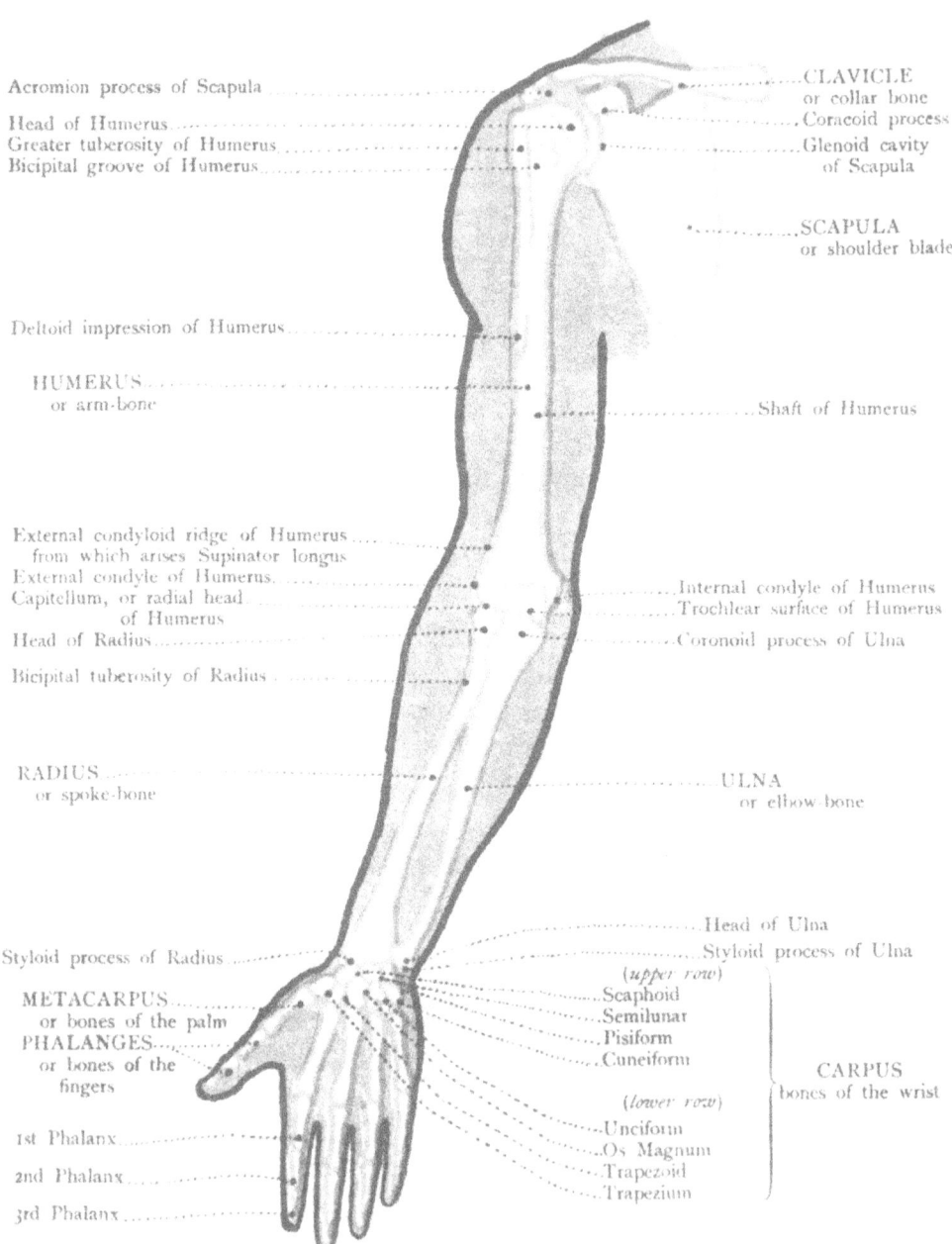

Acromion process of Scapula

Head of Humerus
Greater tuberosity of Humerus
Bicipital groove of Humerus

Deltoid impression of Humerus

HUMERUS
or arm-bone

External condyloid ridge of Humerus
from which arises Supinator longus
External condyle of Humerus
Capitellum, or radial head
of Humerus
Head of Radius

Bicipital tuberosity of Radius

RADIUS
or spoke-bone

Styloid process of Radius

METACARPUS
or bones of the palm
PHALANGES
or bones of the
fingers

1st Phalanx

2nd Phalanx

3rd Phalanx

CLAVICLE
or collar bone
Coracoid process
Glenoid cavity
of Scapula

SCAPULA
or shoulder blade

Shaft of Humerus

Internal condyle of Humerus
Trochlear surface of Humerus
Coronoid process of Ulna

ULNA
or elbow-bone

Head of Ulna
Styloid process of Ulna

(upper row)
Scaphoid
Semilunar
Pisiform
Cuneiform

(lower row)
Unciform
Os Magnum
Trapezoid
Trapezium

CARPUS
bones of the wrist

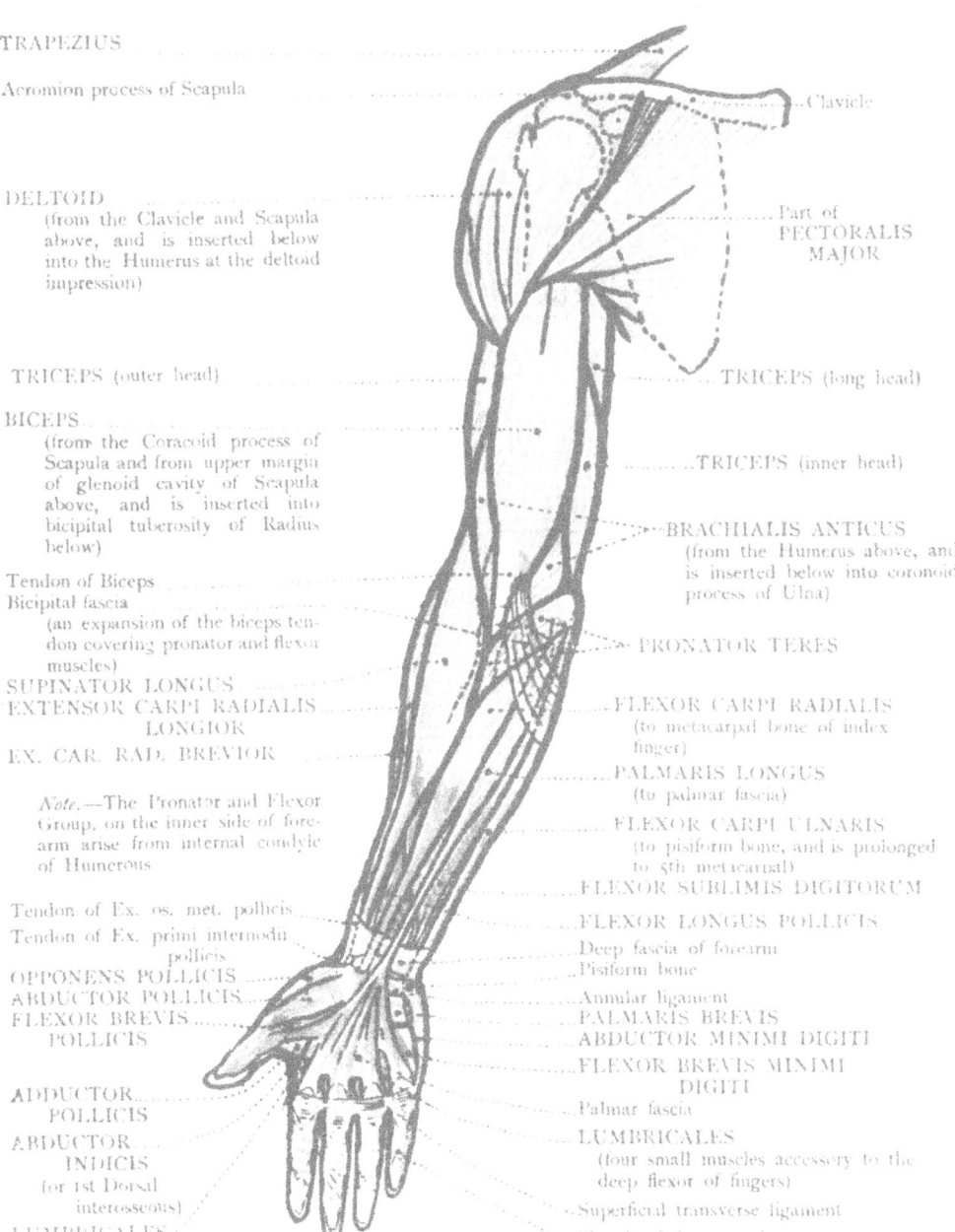

TRAPEZIUS

Acromion process of Scapula

Clavicle

DELTOID
(from the Clavicle and Scapula
above, and is inserted below
into the Humerus at the deltoid
impression)

Part of
PECTORALIS
MAJOR

TRICEPS (outer head)

TRICEPS (long head)

BICEPS
(from the Coracoid process of
Scapula and from upper margin
of glenoid cavity of Scapula
above, and is inserted into
bicipital tuberosity of Radius
below)

TRICEPS (inner head)

BRACHIALIS ANTICUS
(from the Humerus above, and
is inserted below into coronoid
process of Ulna)

Tendon of Biceps
Bicipital fascia
(an expansion of the biceps tendon covering pronator and flexor
muscles)

PRONATOR TERES

SUPINATOR LONGUS
EXTENSOR CARPI RADIALIS
LONGIOR

FLEXOR CARPI RADIALIS
(to metacarpal bone of index
finger)

EX. CAR. RAD. BREVIOR

PALMARIS LONGUS
(to palmar fascia)

*Note.*—The Pronator and Flexor
Group, on the inner side of forearm arise from internal condyle
of Humerous

FLEXOR CARPI ULNARIS
(to pisiform bone, and is prolonged
to 5th metacarpal)

FLEXOR SUBLIMIS DIGITORUM

Tendon of Ex. os. met. pollicis
Tendon of Ex. primi internodii
pollicis

FLEXOR LONGUS POLLICIS
Deep fascia of forearm
Pisiform bone

OPPONENS POLLICIS
ABDUCTOR POLLICIS
FLEXOR BREVIS
POLLICIS

Annular ligament
PALMARIS BREVIS
ABDUCTOR MINIMI DIGITI
FLEXOR BREVIS MINIMI
DIGITI

ADDUCTOR
POLLICIS

Palmar fascia

ABDUCTOR
INDICIS
(or 1st Dorsal
interosseous)

LUMBRICALES
(four small muscles accessory to the
deep flexor of fingers)

Superficial transverse ligament

LUMBRICALES

Sheath of flexor tendons

CLAVICLE

Acromion process of Scapula

Coracoid process
of Scapula

Head of Humerus

SCAPULA

HUMERUS

Internal condyle of Humerus

Trochlea of Humerus

Olecranon process of Ulna

Head of Radius

Coronoid process of Ulna

Bicipital tuberosity

ULNA

RADIUS

Head of Ulna

CARPUS { Scaphoid

Styloid process of Ulna

Trapezium

Semilunar ⎫
Cuneiform ⎬ CARPUS
Pisiform ⎪
Unciform ⎭

1st Metacarpal bone

PHALANGES

5th bone of METACARPUS

1st or proximal ⎫
2nd or middle ⎬
3rd distal, terminal ⎬ PHALANGES
or ungual ⎪
(nail bearing) ⎭

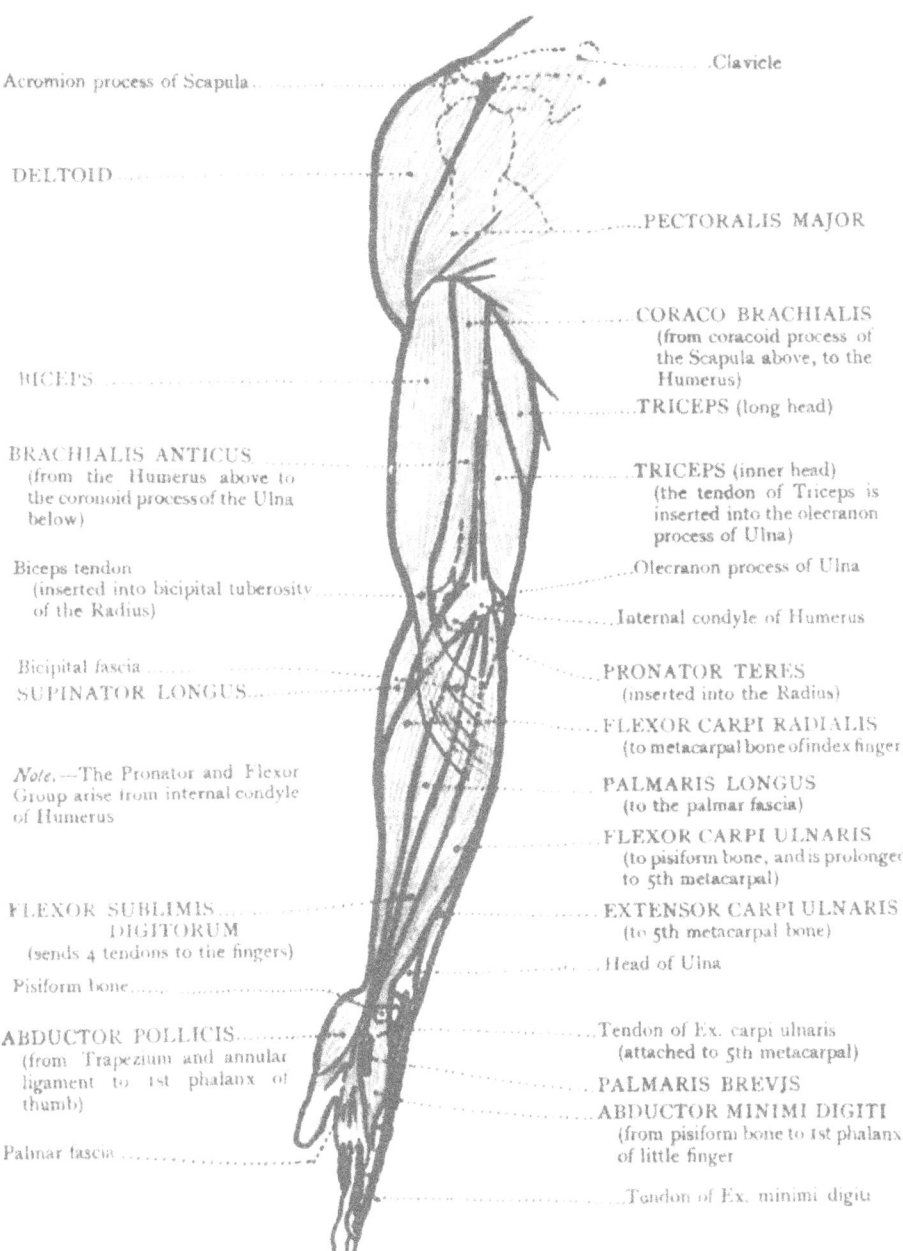

Acromion process of Scapula

Clavicle

DELTOID

PECTORALIS MAJOR

CORACO BRACHIALIS
(from coracoid process of
the Scapula above, to the
Humerus)

BICEPS

TRICEPS (long head)

BRACHIALIS ANTICUS
(from the Humerus above to
the coronoid process of the Ulna
below)

TRICEPS (inner head)
(the tendon of Triceps is
inserted into the olecranon
process of Ulna)

Biceps tendon
(inserted into bicipital tuberosity
of the Radius)

Olecranon process of Ulna

Internal condyle of Humerus

Bicipital fascia

SUPINATOR LONGUS

PRONATOR TERES
(inserted into the Radius)

FLEXOR CARPI RADIALIS
(to metacarpal bone of index finger)

Note.—The Pronator and Flexor
Group arise from internal condyle
of Humerus

PALMARIS LONGUS
(to the palmar fascia)

FLEXOR CARPI ULNARIS
(to pisiform bone, and is prolonged
to 5th metacarpal)

FLEXOR SUBLIMIS
DIGITORUM
(sends 4 tendons to the fingers)

EXTENSOR CARPI ULNARIS
(to 5th metacarpal bone)

Pisiform bone

Head of Ulna

ABDUCTOR POLLICIS
(from Trapezium and annular
ligament to 1st phalanx of
thumb)

Tendon of Ex. carpi ulnaris
(attached to 5th metacarpal)

PALMARIS BREVIS

ABDUCTOR MINIMI DIGITI
(from pisiform bone to 1st phalanx
of little finger

Palmar fascia

Tendon of Ex. minimi digiti

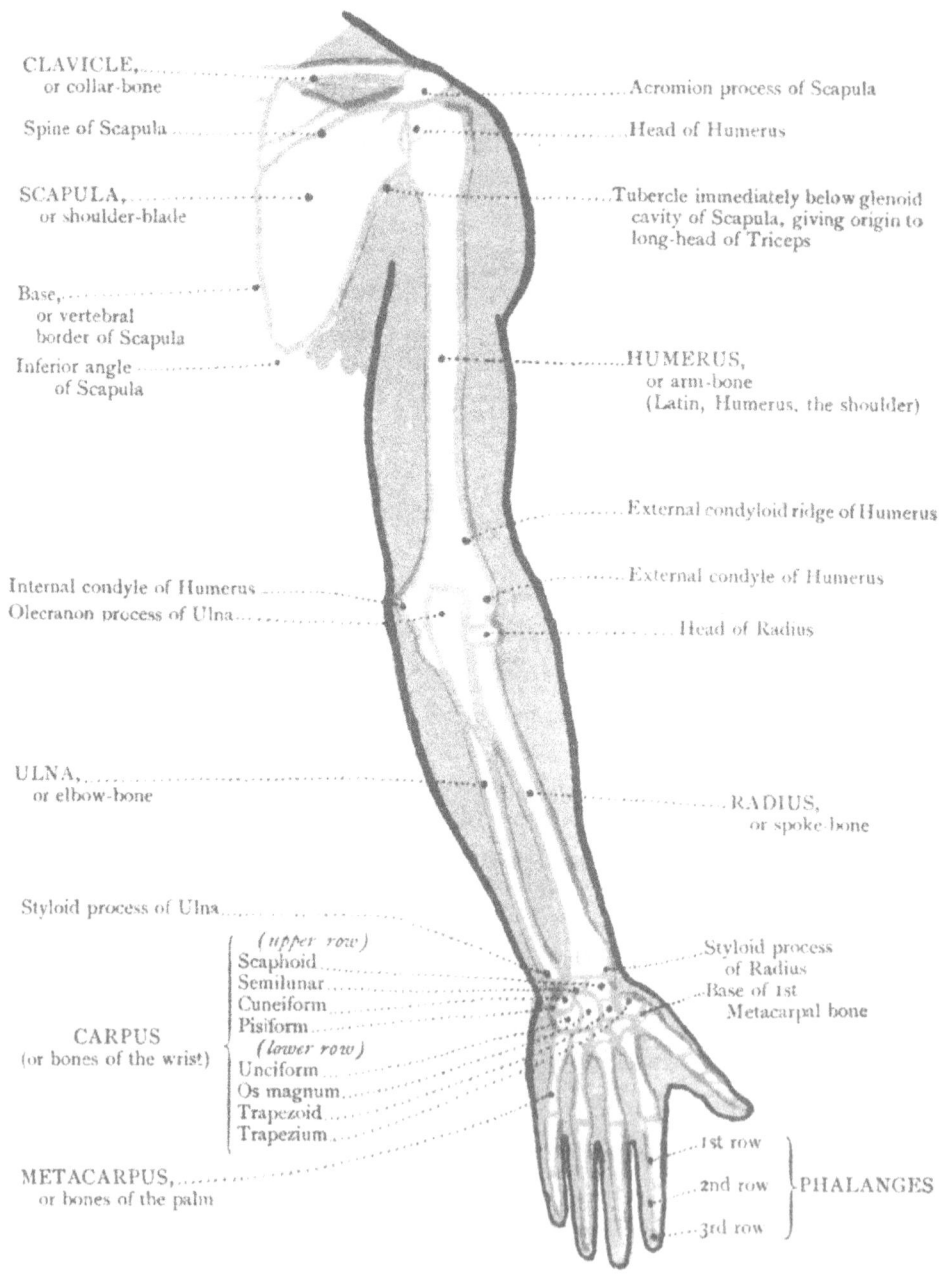

CLAVICLE,
  or collar-bone

Acromion process of Scapula

Spine of Scapula

Head of Humerus

SCAPULA,
  or shoulder-blade

Tubercle immediately below glenoid
cavity of Scapula, giving origin to
long-head of Triceps

Base,
  or vertebral
  border of Scapula

Inferior angle
  of Scapula

HUMERUS,
  or arm-bone
  (Latin, Humerus, the shoulder)

External condyloid ridge of Humerus

Internal condyle of Humerus

External condyle of Humerus

Olecranon process of Ulna

Head of Radius

ULNA,
  or elbow-bone

RADIUS,
  or spoke-bone

Styloid process of Ulna

Styloid process
  of Radius

(upper row)
Scaphoid
Semilunar
Cuneiform
Pisiform

Base of 1st
  Metacarpal bone

CARPUS
(or bones of the wrist)

(lower row)
Unciform
Os magnum
Trapezoid
Trapezium

METACARPUS,
  or bones of the palm

1st row

2nd row

PHALANGES

3rd row

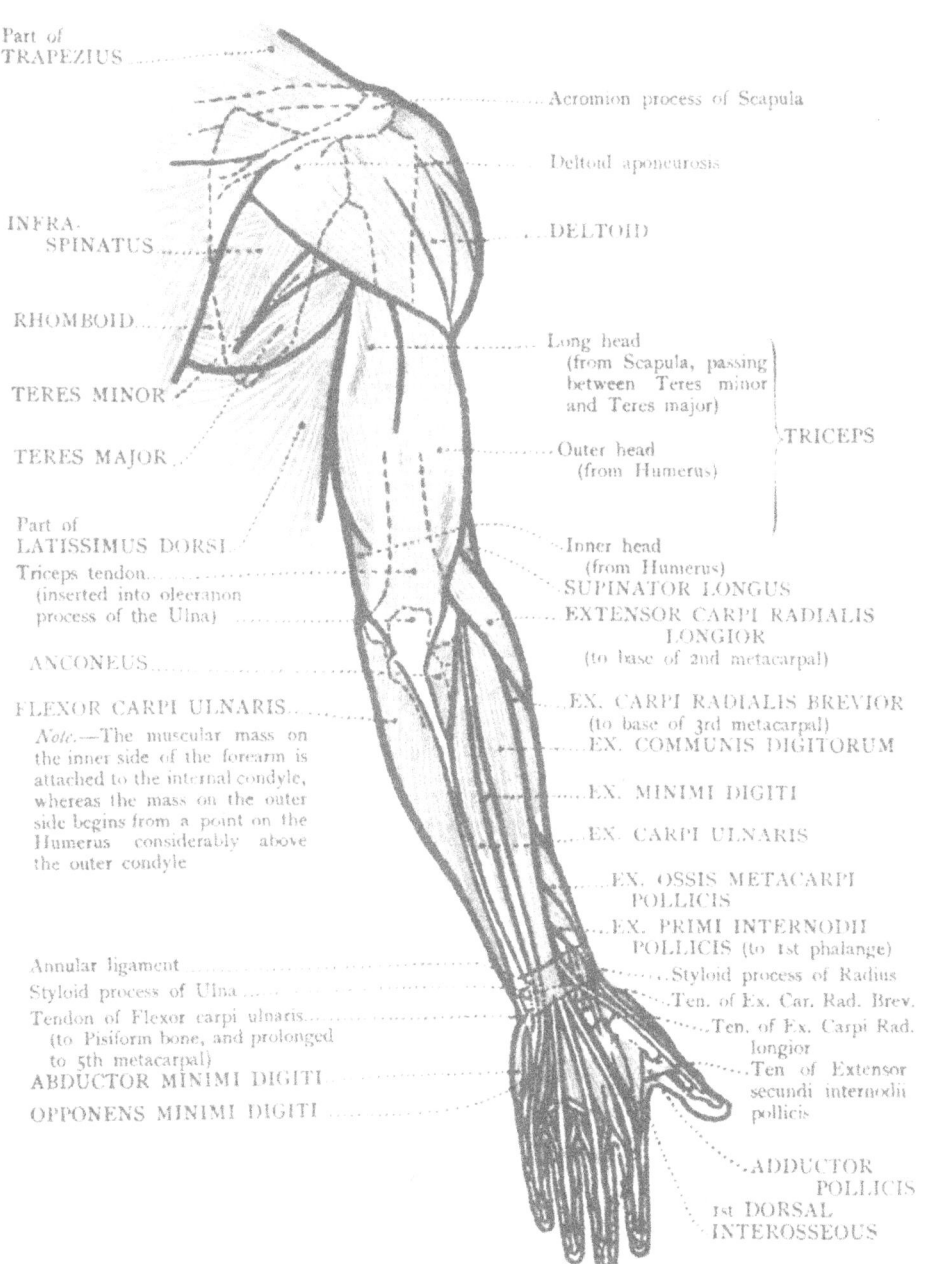

Part of
TRAPEZIUS

Acromion process of Scapula

Deltoid aponeurosis

INFRA-
SPINATUS

DELTOID

RHOMBOID

Long head
(from Scapula, passing
between Teres minor
and Teres major)

TERES MINOR

TERES MAJOR

Outer head
(from Humerus)

TRICEPS

Part of
LATISSIMUS DORSI

Inner head
(from Humerus)

Triceps tendon
(inserted into olecranon
process of the Ulna)

SUPINATOR LONGUS

EXTENSOR CARPI RADIALIS
LONGIOR
(to base of 2nd metacarpal)

ANCONEUS

EX. CARPI RADIALIS BREVIOR
(to base of 3rd metacarpal)

FLEXOR CARPI ULNARIS

EX. COMMUNIS DIGITORUM

Note.—The muscular mass on
the inner side of the forearm is
attached to the internal condyle,
whereas the mass on the outer
side begins from a point on the
Humerus considerably above
the outer condyle

EX. MINIMI DIGITI

EX. CARPI ULNARIS

EX. OSSIS METACARPI
POLLICIS

EX. PRIMI INTERNODII
POLLICIS (to 1st phalange)

Annular ligament

Styloid process of Radius

Styloid process of Ulna

Ten. of Ex. Car. Rad. Brev.

Tendon of Flexor carpi ulnaris
(to Pisiform bone, and prolonged
to 5th metacarpal)

Ten. of Ex. Carpi Rad.
longior

ABDUCTOR MINIMI DIGITI

Ten of Extensor
secundi internodii
pollicis

OPPONENS MINIMI DIGITI

ADDUCTOR
POLLICIS

1st DORSAL
INTEROSSEOUS

# THE BONES IN RELATION TO THE OUTLINE OF FIGURE
## FRONT VIEW

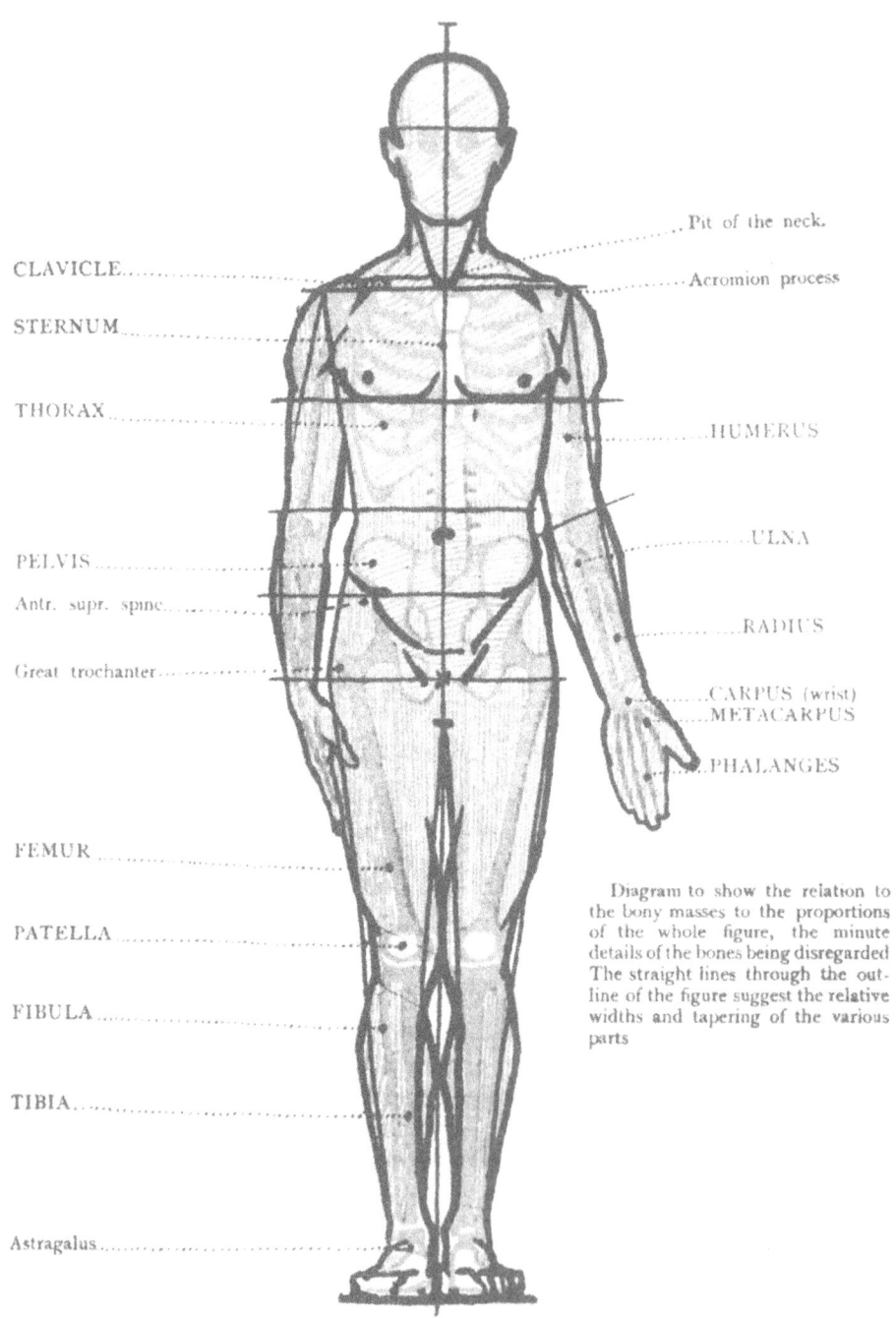

Pit of the neck.

CLAVICLE

Acromion process

STERNUM

THORAX

HUMERUS

ULNA

PELVIS

Antr. supr. spine

RADIUS

Great trochanter

CARPUS (wrist)
METACARPUS

PHALANGES

FEMUR

Diagram to show the relation to
the bony masses to the proportions
of the whole figure, the minute
details of the bones being disregarded
The straight lines through the outline of the figure suggest the relative
widths and tapering of the various
parts

PATELLA

FIBULA

TIBIA

Astragalus

28

# CONSTRUCTION LINES OF THE STANDING FIGURE.
## FRONT VIEW.

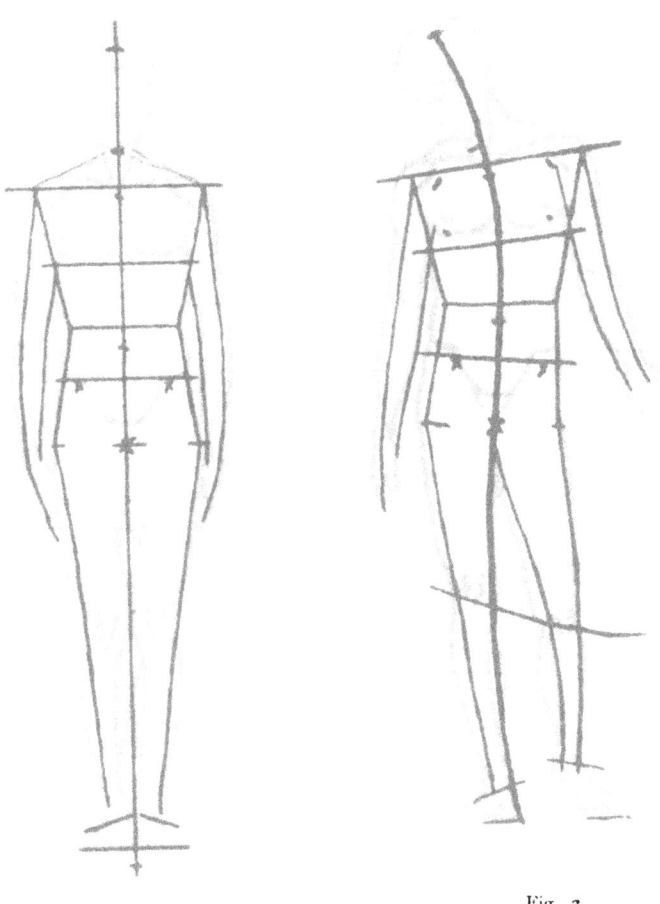

Fig. 1

Fig. 2

In the above diagrams, Fig. 1 shows the leading constructive lines when the figure is standing upright and resting on both legs. In this position the line passing through the shoulders, and that drawn across the antr. supr. spines of the Pelvis, are both obviously at right angles to the vertical axis of the body.

In Figure 2 the weight of the body is carried mainly on one leg, and in this position the axial line of the body becomes a curve, but still the line drawn through the shoulders and that through the Pelvis may be regarded as at right angles to this imaginary curve. Observe that the Pelvis is higher on the side which supports the figure, and also that the hip makes a sharper angle on that side, and further, note the slope of the standing leg with the ground, necessary for the balance of the figure.

The axial line of the body carried down through the standing leg gives here a line of double curvature, which is the first line to be drawn in suggesting the pose.

# THE BONES IN RELATION TO OUTLINE OF FIGURE.
## BACK VIEW.

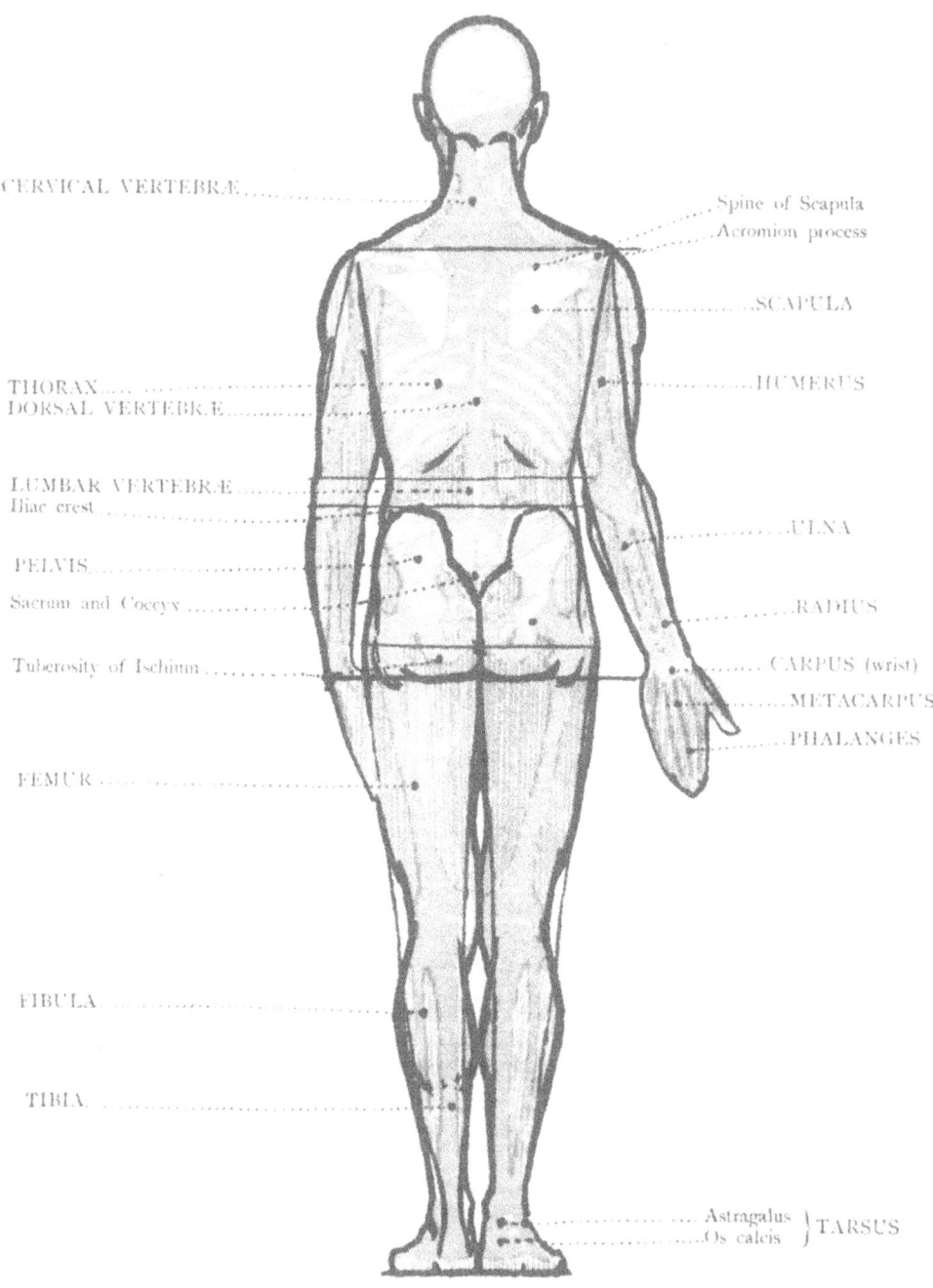

CERVICAL VERTEBRÆ

Spine of Scapula

Acromion process

SCAPULA

THORAX

HUMERUS

DORSAL VERTEBRÆ

LUMBAR VERTEBRÆ

Iliac crest

ULNA

PELVIS

Sacrum and Coccyx

RADIUS

Tuberosity of Ischium

CARPUS (wrist)

METACARPUS

PHALANGES

FEMUR

FIBULA

TIBIA

Astragalus

Os calcis

TARSUS

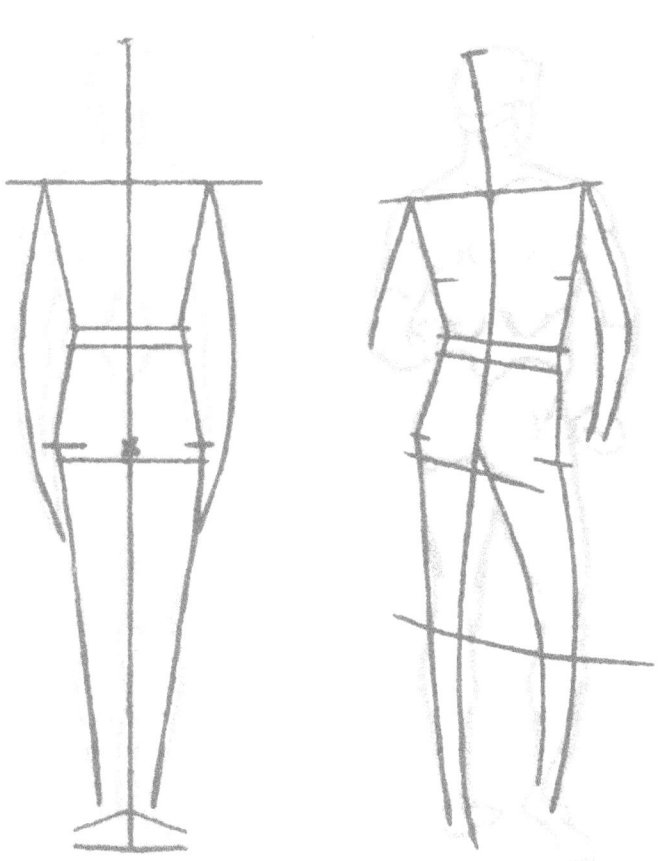

The above diagrams show the leading constructive lines of the back view of tl
similar positions to those already shown in the front view. The greater length ot the trunk
as viewed from behind will be observed on comparison with the front view. The lines
across the back are drawn through the shoulders, the lower end of the thorax, the iliac
crests, and the gluteal fold.

# THE BONES IN RELATION TO OUTLINE OF FIGURE.
## SIDE VIEW.

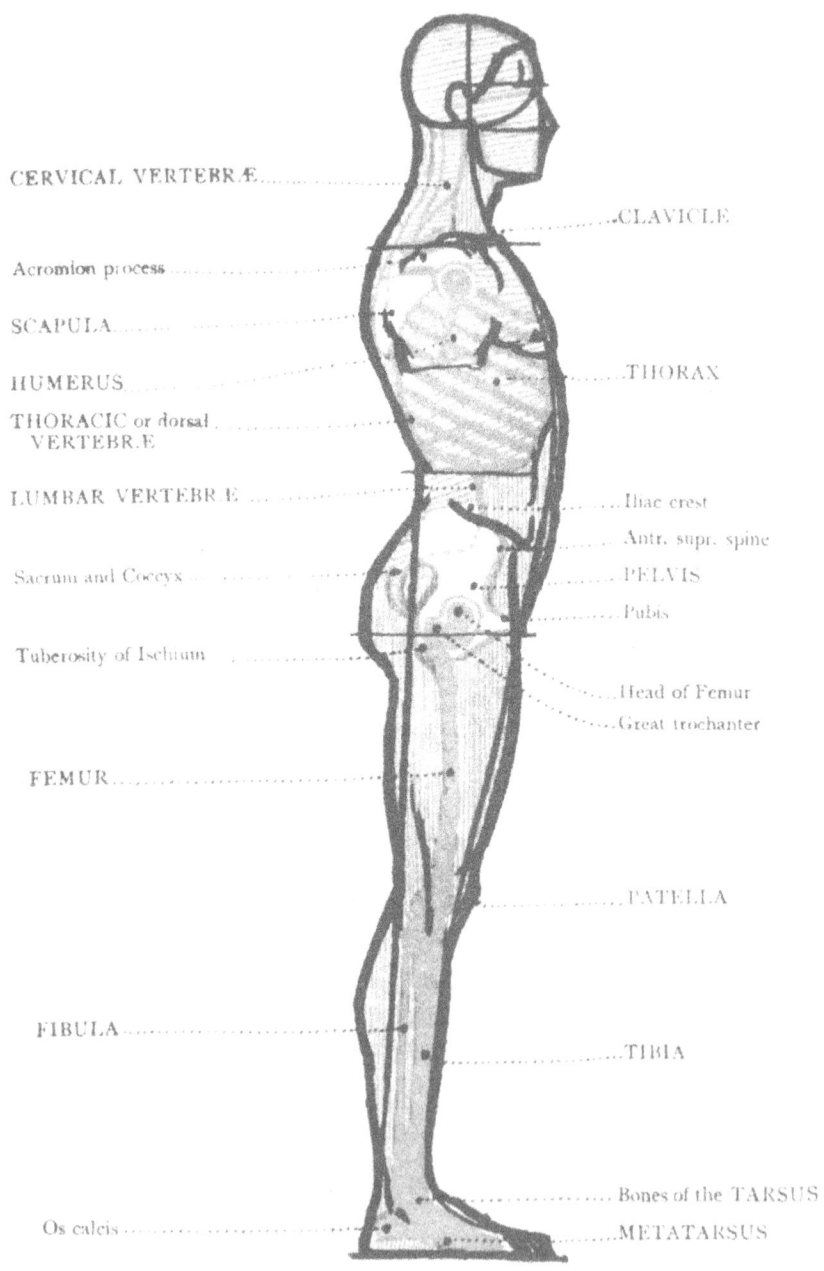

CERVICAL VERTEBRÆ

CLAVICLE

Acromion process

SCAPULA

HUMERUS

THORAX

THORACIC or dorsal
VERTEBRÆ

LUMBAR VERTEBRÆ

Iliac crest

Antr. supr. spine

Sacrum and Coccyx

PELVIS

Pubis

Tuberosity of Ischium

Head of Femur

Great trochanter

FEMUR

PATELLA

FIBULA

TIBIA

Bones of the TARSUS

Os calcis

METATARSUS

# PARTS OF THE BONES WHICH DIRECTLY AFFECT
## THE SURFACE FORM—SIDE VIEW.

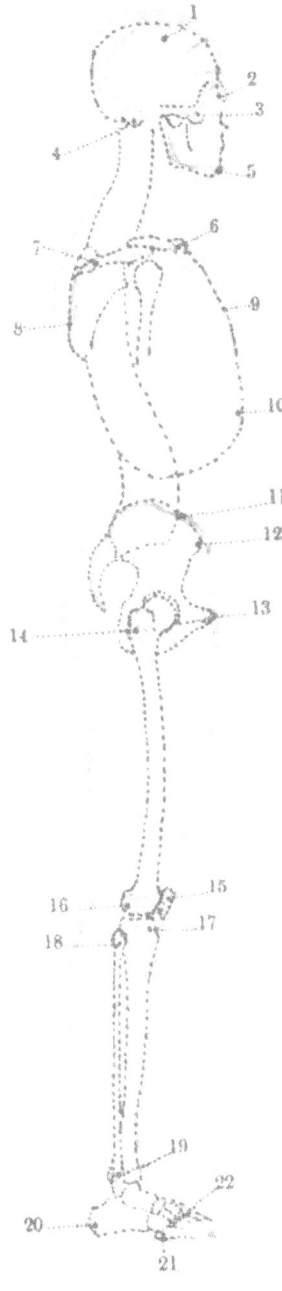

References to the bones

### HEAD

1. Bones of the cranium; the shaded part is more or less plainly revealed upon the surface
2. Nasal bone
3. Malar or cheek-bone and Zygomatic arch
4. Mastoid process of Temporal bone
5. Lower jaw-bone, outline of its entire length

### TRUNK

6. Clavicle
7. Spine of Scapula
8. Base of Scapula
9. Sternum
10. Cartilages of Ribs
11. Iliac Crest
12. Anterior superior iliac spine
13. Pubis

### LOWER LIMB

14. Great trochanter of Femur
15. Patella
16. Outer condyle of Femur
17. Head of Tibia
18. Head of Fibula
19. Outer malleolus of Fibula
20. Os Calcis
21. Tuberosity of 5th metatarsal
22. Metatarsal bones

NOTE.—The parts of the Bones and Cartilages which are subcutaneous, or sufficiently near the surface to affect the surface form, are in this diagram marked in blue.

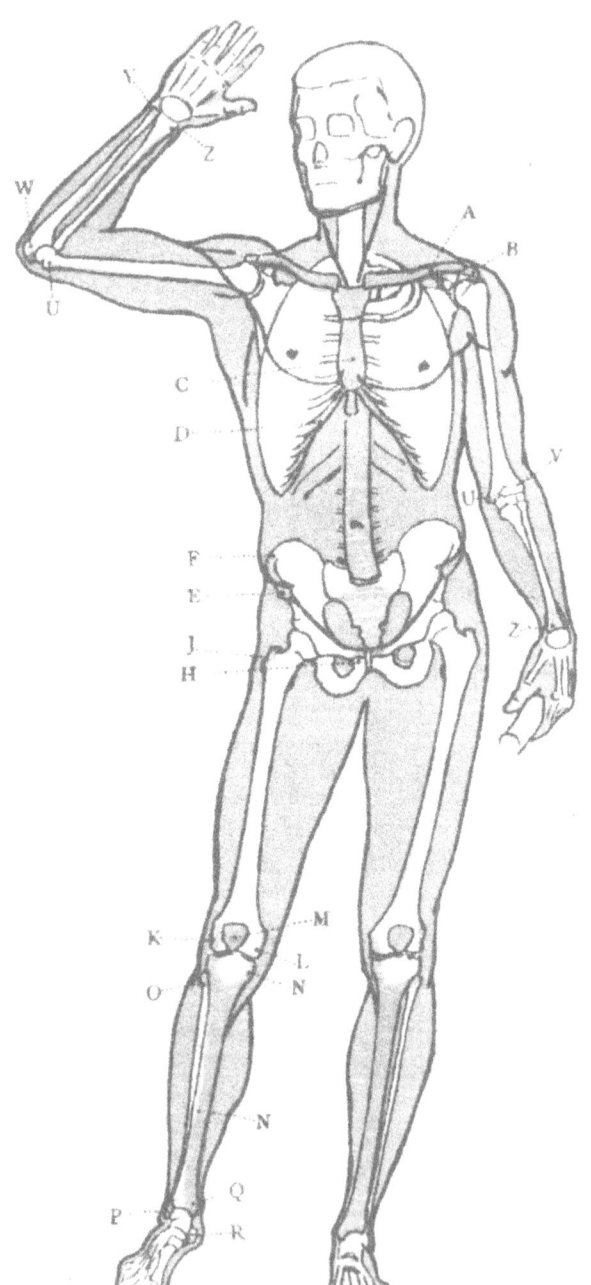

References to the Bones and Cartilages in the three views of the figure in action.

## TRUNK.

A—Clavicle
B—Acromion process of Scapula
B'—Spine of Scapula
B"—Base of Scapula
C—Sternum
D—Cartilages of the Ribs
E—Anterior superior iliac spine
F—Iliac crest
G—Posterior superior iliac spine
H—Pubis
I—Sacrum

## LOWER LIMB.

J—Great trochanter of Femur
K—Outer condyle of Femur
L—Inner condyle of Femur
M—Patella
N—Head of Tibia
N'—Shaft of Tibia
O—Head of Fibula
P—Outer malleolus of Fibula
Q—Inner malleolus of Tibia
R—Os Calcis
S—Tuberosity of 5th metatarsal
T—Ball of great toe

## UPPER LIMB.

U—Inner condyle of Humerus
V—Outer condyle of Humerus
W—Olecranon process of Ulna
X—Posterior border of Ulna
Y—Head and styloid process of Ulna
Z—Styloid process of Radius

NOTE.—The parts of the Bones and Cartilages which are subcutaneous or sufficiently near the surface to affect the surface form directly, are, in this diagram marked in blue. The parts so marked are therefore of great importance in sketching out the masses of the figure.

# THE MUSCLES AS IN ACTION—Front View.

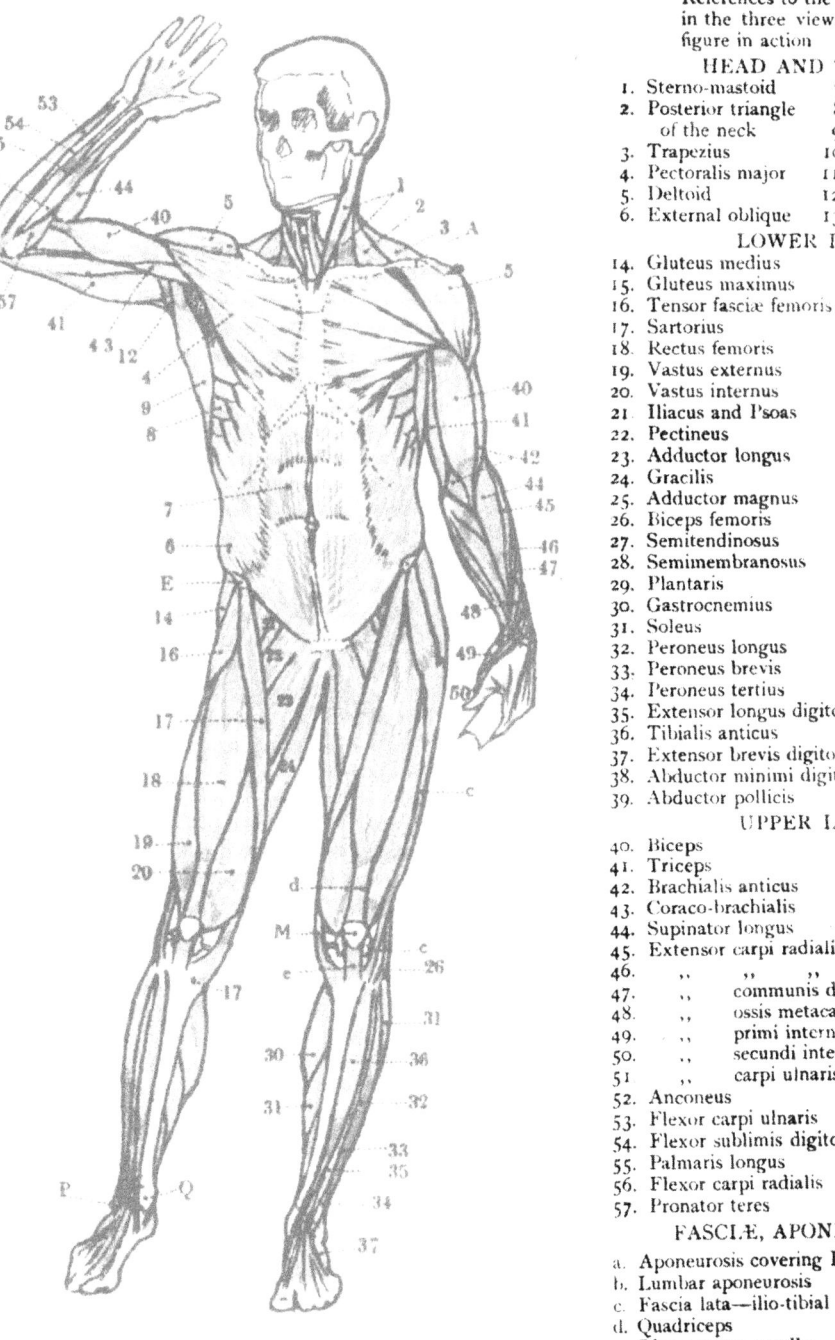

# THE BONES AS IN ACTION.—Back View.

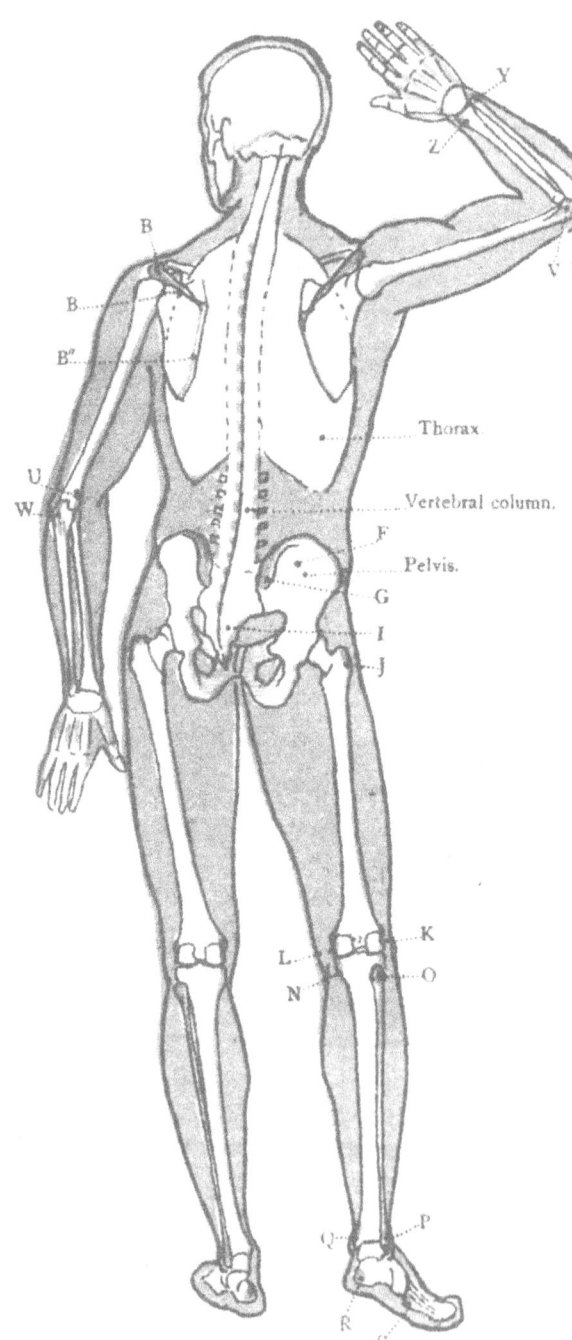

References to the Bones and Cartilages in the three views of the figure in action.

## TRUNK.

A—Clavicle
B—Acromion process of Scapula
B'—Spine of Scapula
B"—Base of Scapula
·C—Sternum
D—Cartilages of the Ribs
E—Anterior superior iliac spine
F—Iliac crest
G—Posterior superior iliac spine
H—Pubis
I—Sacrum

## LOWER LIMB.

J—Great trochanter of Femur
K—Outer condyle of Femur
L—Inner condyle of Femur
M—Patella
N—Head of Tibia
N'—Shaft of Tibia
O—Head of Fibula
P—Outer malleolus of Fibula
Q—Inner malleolus of Tibia
R—Os Calcis
S—Tuberosity of 5th metatarsal
T—Ball of great toe

## UPPER LIMB.

U—Inner condyle of Humerus
V—Outer condyle of Humerus
W—Olecranon process of Ulna
X—Posterior border of Ulna
Y—Head and styloid process of
        Ulna
Z—Styloid process of Radius

NOTE.—The parts of the Bones and Cartilages which are subcutaneous or sufficiently near the surface to affect the surface form directly, are, in this diagram marked in blue. The parts so marked are therefore of great importance in sketching out the masses of the figure.

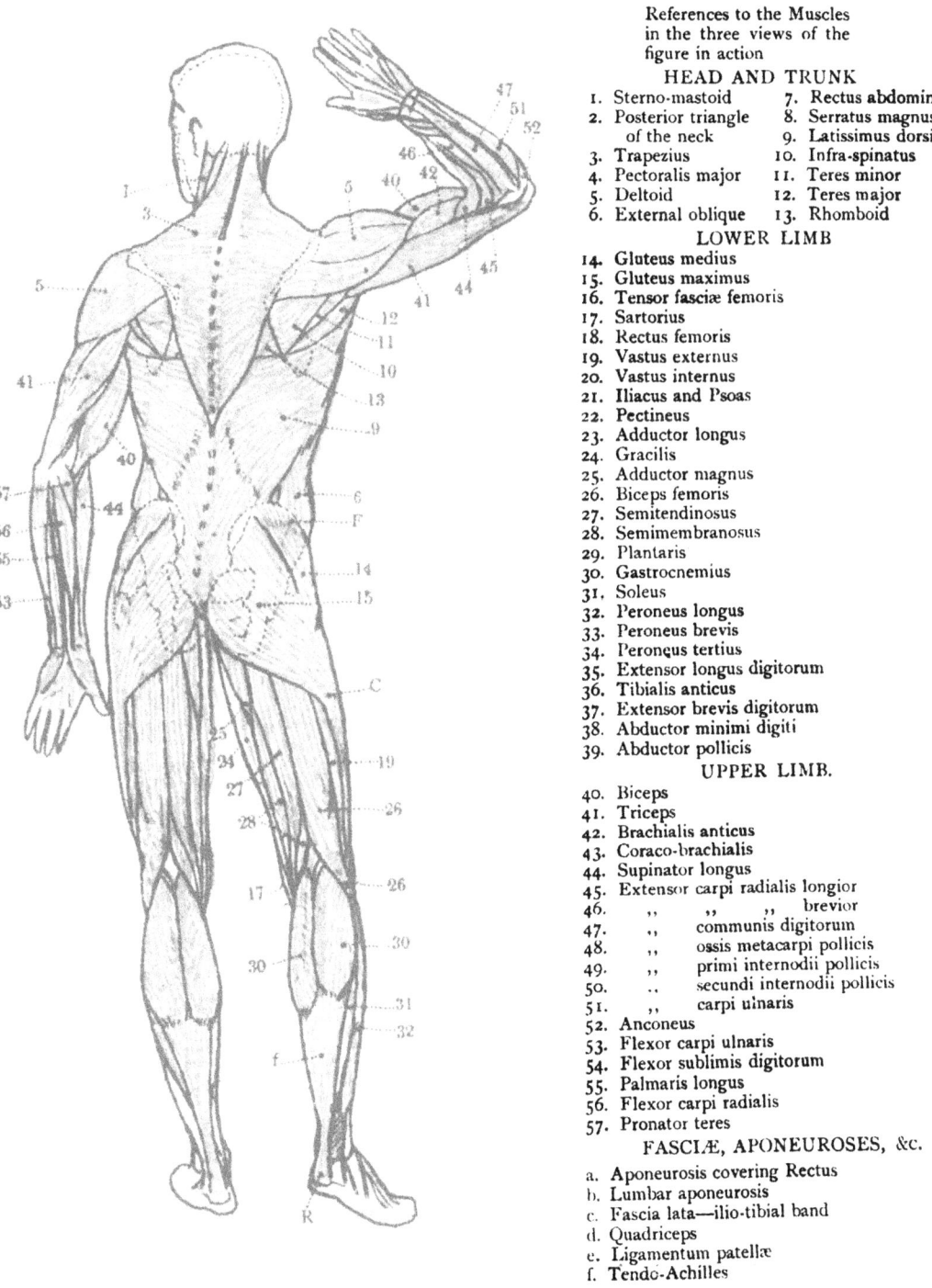

References to the Muscles
in the three views of the
figure in action

### HEAD AND TRUNK

1. Sterno-mastoid
2. Posterior triangle of the neck
3. Trapezius
4. Pectoralis major
5. Deltoid
6. External oblique
7. Rectus abdominis
8. Serratus magnus
9. Latissimus dorsi
10. Infra-spinatus
11. Teres minor
12. Teres major
13. Rhomboid

### LOWER LIMB

14. Gluteus medius
15. Gluteus maximus
16. Tensor fasciæ femoris
17. Sartorius
18. Rectus femoris
19. Vastus externus
20. Vastus internus
21. Iliacus and Psoas
22. Pectineus
23. Adductor longus
24. Gracilis
25. Adductor magnus
26. Biceps femoris
27. Semitendinosus
28. Semimembranosus
29. Plantaris
30. Gastrocnemius
31. Soleus
32. Peroneus longus
33. Peroneus brevis
34. Peroneus tertius
35. Extensor longus digitorum
36. Tibialis anticus
37. Extensor brevis digitorum
38. Abductor minimi digiti
39. Abductor pollicis

### UPPER LIMB.

40. Biceps
41. Triceps
42. Brachialis anticus
43. Coraco-brachialis
44. Supinator longus
45. Extensor carpi radialis longior
46. ,,   ,,   ,,   brevior
47. ,,   communis digitorum
48. ,,   ossis metacarpi pollicis
49. ,,   primi internodii pollicis
50. ..   secundi internodii pollicis
51. ,,   carpi ulnaris
52. Anconeus
53. Flexor carpi ulnaris
54. Flexor sublimis digitorum
55. Palmaris longus
56. Flexor carpi radialis
57. Pronator teres

### FASCIÆ, APONEUROSES, &c.

a. Aponeurosis covering Rectus
b. Lumbar aponeurosis
c. Fascia lata—ilio-tibial band
d. Quadriceps
e. Ligamentum patellæ
f. Tendo-Achilles

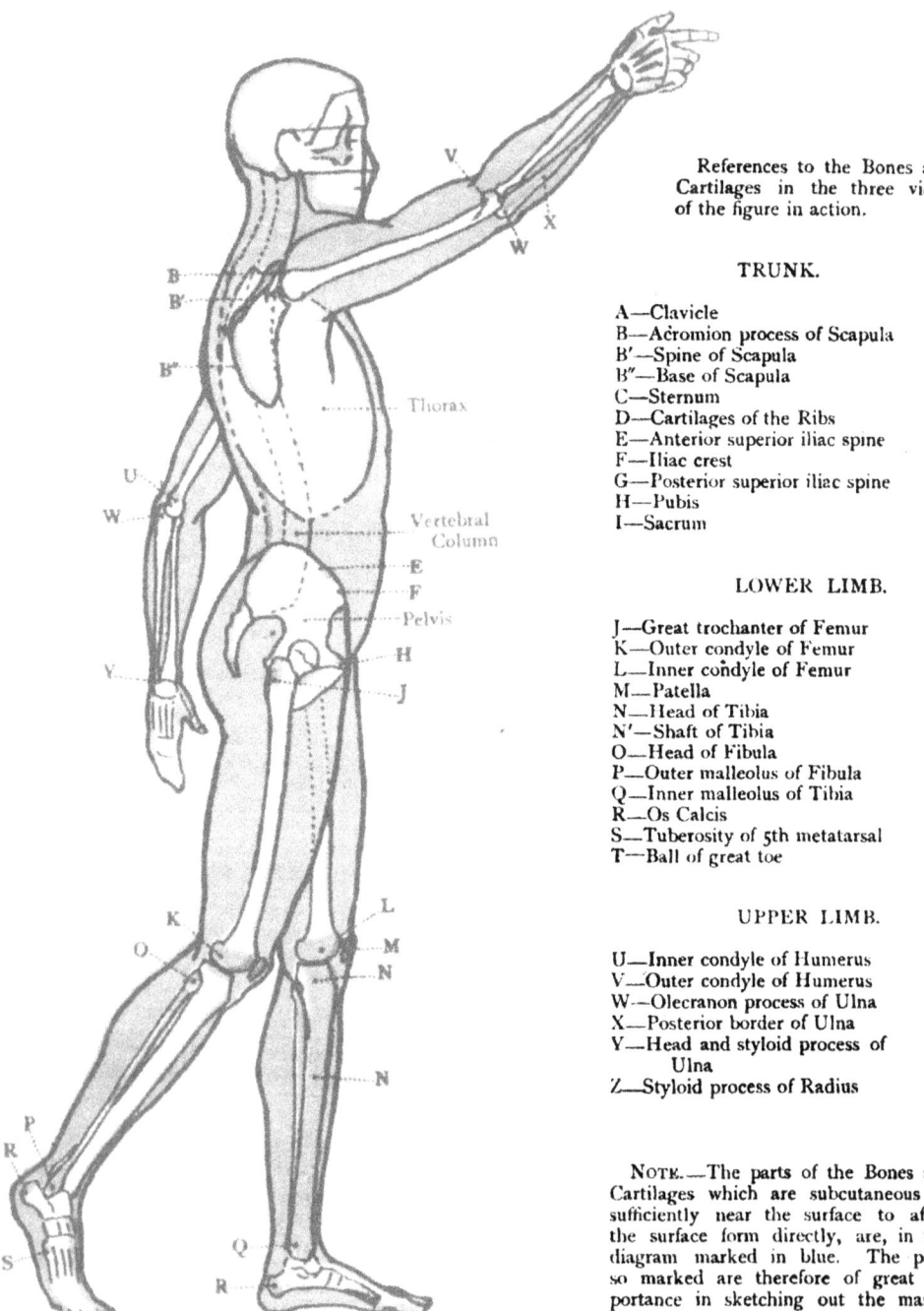

References to the Bones and Cartilages in the three views of the figure in action.

## TRUNK.

A—Clavicle
B—Acromion process of Scapula
B'—Spine of Scapula
B"—Base of Scapula
C—Sternum
D—Cartilages of the Ribs
E—Anterior superior iliac spine
F—Iliac crest
G—Posterior superior iliac spine
H—Pubis
I—Sacrum

## LOWER LIMB.

J—Great trochanter of Femur
K—Outer condyle of Femur
L—Inner condyle of Femur
M—Patella
N—Head of Tibia
N'—Shaft of Tibia
O—Head of Fibula
P—Outer malleolus of Fibula
Q—Inner malleolus of Tibia
R—Os Calcis
S—Tuberosity of 5th metatarsal
T—Ball of great toe

## UPPER LIMB.

U—Inner condyle of Humerus
V—Outer condyle of Humerus
W—Olecranon process of Ulna
X—Posterior border of Ulna
Y—Head and styloid process of Ulna
Z—Styloid process of Radius

NOTE.—The parts of the Bones and Cartilages which are subcutaneous or sufficiently near the surface to affect the surface form directly, are, in this diagram marked in blue. The parts so marked are therefore of great importance in sketching out the masses of the figure.

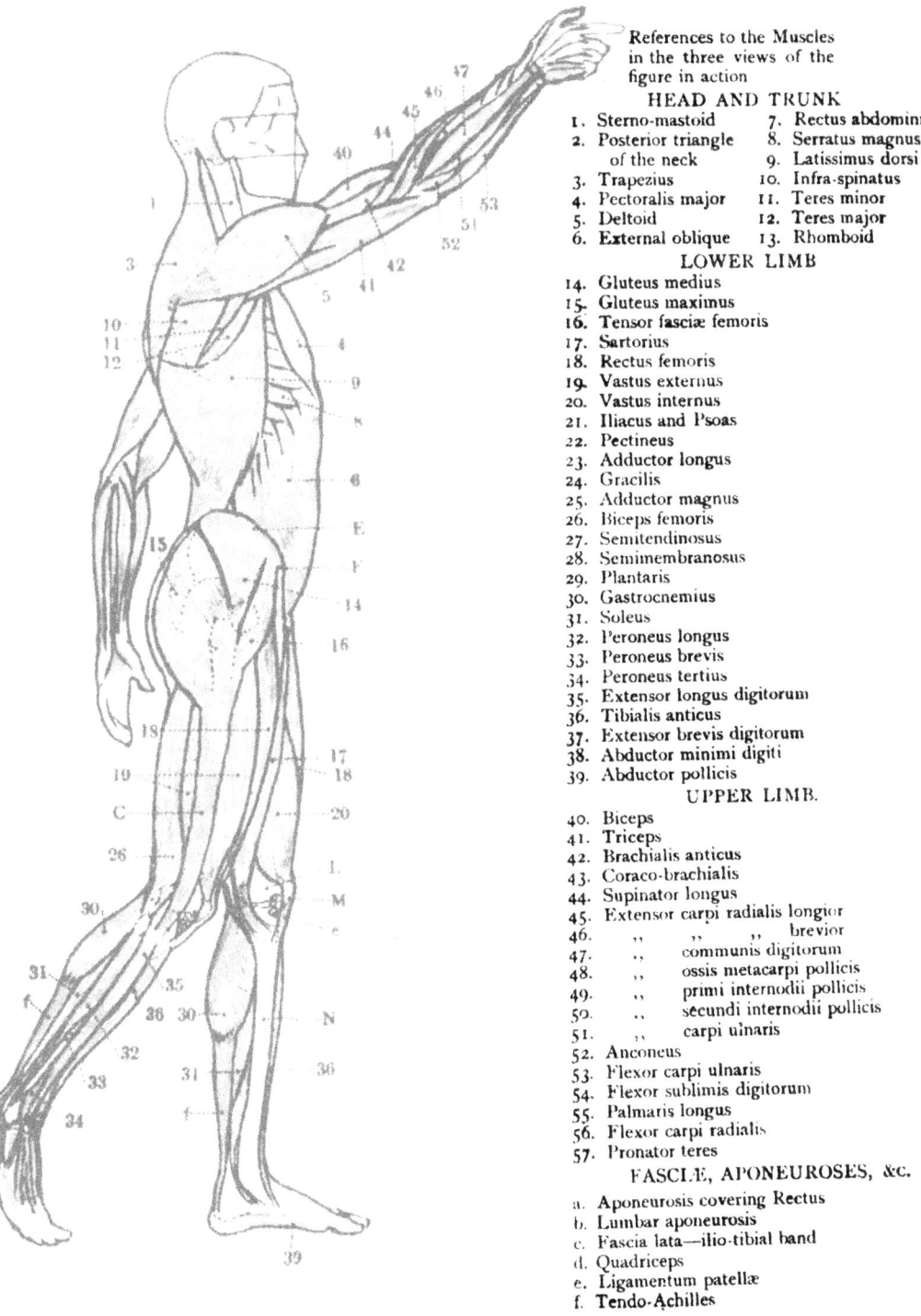

References to the Muscles
in the three views of the
figure in action

### HEAD AND TRUNK

| | |
|---|---|
| 1. Sterno-mastoid | 7. Rectus abdominis |
| 2. Posterior triangle | 8. Serratus magnus |
| of the neck | 9. Latissimus dorsi |
| 3. Trapezius | 10. Infra-spinatus |
| 4. Pectoralis major | 11. Teres minor |
| 5. Deltoid | 12. Teres major |
| 6. External oblique | 13. Rhomboid |

### LOWER LIMB

14. Gluteus medius
15. Gluteus maximus
16. Tensor fasciæ femoris
17. Sartorius
18. Rectus femoris
19. Vastus externus
20. Vastus internus
21. Iliacus and Psoas
22. Pectineus
23. Adductor longus
24. Gracilis
25. Adductor magnus
26. Biceps femoris
27. Semitendinosus
28. Semimembranosus
29. Plantaris
30. Gastrocnemius
31. Soleus
32. Peroneus longus
33. Peroneus brevis
34. Peroneus tertius
35. Extensor longus digitorum
36. Tibialis anticus
37. Extensor brevis digitorum
38. Abductor minimi digiti
39. Abductor pollicis

### UPPER LIMB.

40. Biceps
41. Triceps
42. Brachialis anticus
43. Coraco-brachialis
44. Supinator longus
45. Extensor carpi radialis longior
46. ,, ,, ,, brevior
47. ,, communis digitorum
48. ,, ossis metacarpi pollicis
49. ,, primi internodii pollicis
50. ,, secundi internodii pollicis
51. ,, carpi ulnaris
52. Anconeus
53. Flexor carpi ulnaris
54. Flexor sublimis digitorum
55. Palmaris longus
56. Flexor carpi radialis
57. Pronator teres

### FASCIÆ, APONEUROSES, &c.

a. Aponeurosis covering Rectus
b. Lumbar aponeurosis
c. Fascia lata—ilio-tibial band
d. Quadriceps
e. Ligamentum patellæ
f. Tendo-Achilles

# DETAILS OF THE FACE.

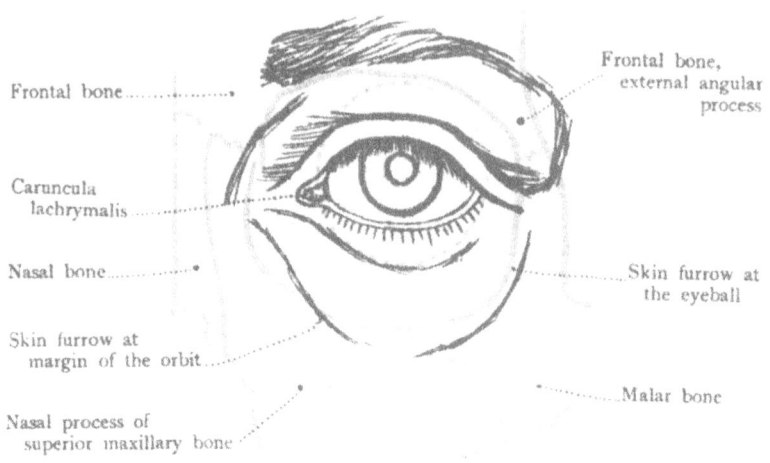

Frontal bone...........

Frontal bone, external angular process

Caruncula lachrymalis ........

Nasal bone...........

Skin furrow at the eyeball

Skin furrow at margin of the orbit ........

Malar bone

Nasal process of superior maxillary bone

## CARTILAGES OF THE NOSE.

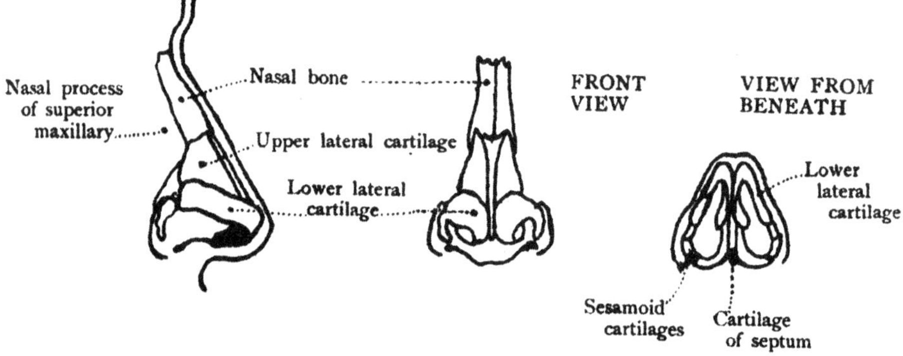

Nasal process of superior maxillary........

Nasal bone ...........

Upper lateral cartilage

Lower lateral cartilage........

**FRONT VIEW**

**VIEW FROM BENEATH**

Lower lateral cartilage

Sesamoid cartilages

Cartilage of septum

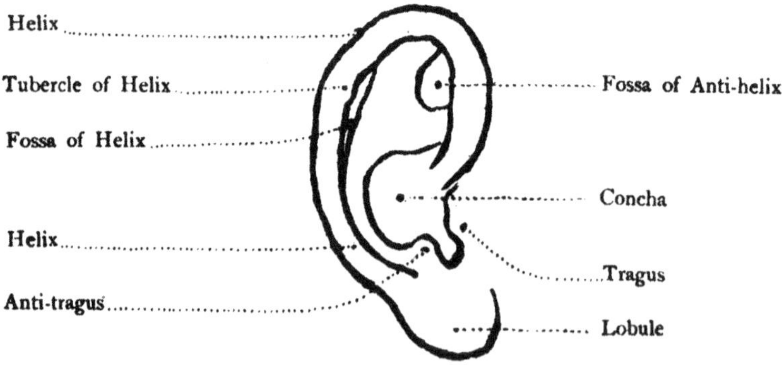

Helix ...........

Tubercle of Helix ........

Fossa of Anti-helix

Fossa of Helix ........

Helix...........

Concha

Tragus

Anti-tragus ........

Lobule

# MUSCLES OF THE HEAD.

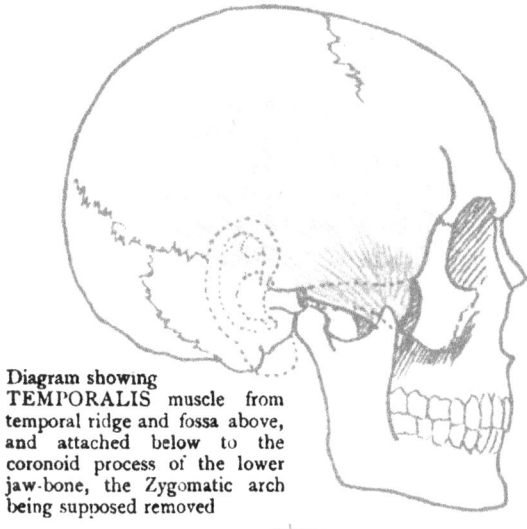

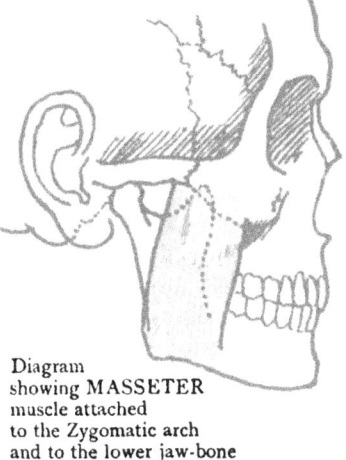

Diagram showing
TEMPORALIS muscle from
temporal ridge and fossa above,
and attached below to the
coronoid process of the lower
jaw-bone, the Zygomatic arch
being supposed removed

Diagram
showing MASSETER
muscle attached
to the Zygomatic arch
and to the lower jaw-bone

References to muscles of the face

1. ORBICULARIS PALPEBRARUM
   from the tendo-palpebrarum, the frontal
   bone and superior maxillary, at the inner
   margin of orbit; it blends with occipito-
   frontalis and other muscles

2. CORRUGATOR SUPERCILII
   from frontal bone at the internal angular
   process; it blends with occipito-frontalis

3. PYRAMIDALIS NASI
   a small slip prolonged downwards from
   the occipito-frontalis to the nasal bones

4. COMPRESSOR NARIS
   from superior maxillary bone to the cartilage
   of the wing of the nose, and expands to
   the bridge of the nose

5. LEVATOR LABII SUPERIORIS
   ALÆQUE NASI from superior maxillary
   to cartilage of nose and to the upper lip

6. ORBICULARIS ORIS,
   the oval muscle which forms the chief mass
   of the lips

   The following muscles are inserted into
   the muscular substance of the lips

7. LEVATOR LABII SUPERIORIS
   from the superior maxillary and the malar
   bone to the upper lip

8. LEVATOR ANGULI ORIS
   from superior maxillary to corner of mouth

9. ZYGOMATICUS MINOR ⎫ from malar
10. ,, MAJOR ⎬ bone to corner
   ⎭ of mouth

11. BUCCINATOR
    from both superior and inferior maxillary
    bones to the corner of the mouth

12. DEPRESSOR ANGULI ORIS
    from inferior maxillary to corner of mouth

13. DEPRESSOR LABII INFERIORIS
    from inferior maxillary to lower lip

14. LEVATOR MENTI
    from inferior maxillary to the integument
    of the chin

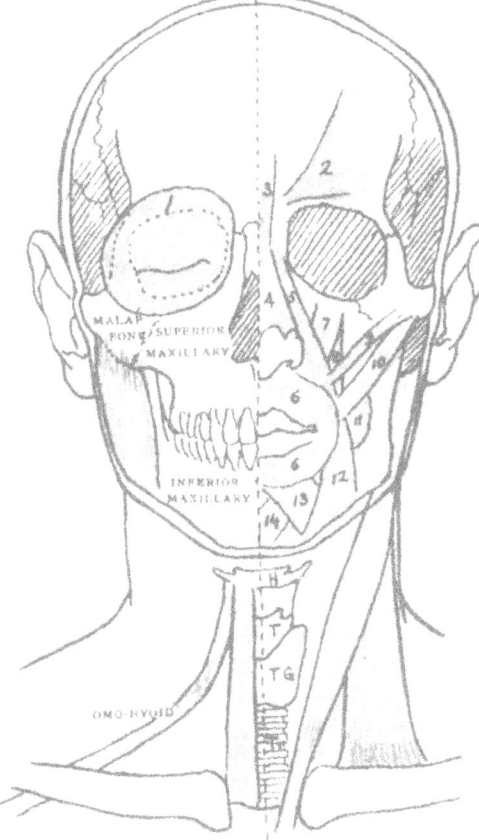

H. Hyoid bone
T. Thyroid cartilage of the Larynx
    (Pomum Adami)
T.G. Thyroid gland
Tr. Trachea or windpipe

41

# MUSCLES OF THE NECK..

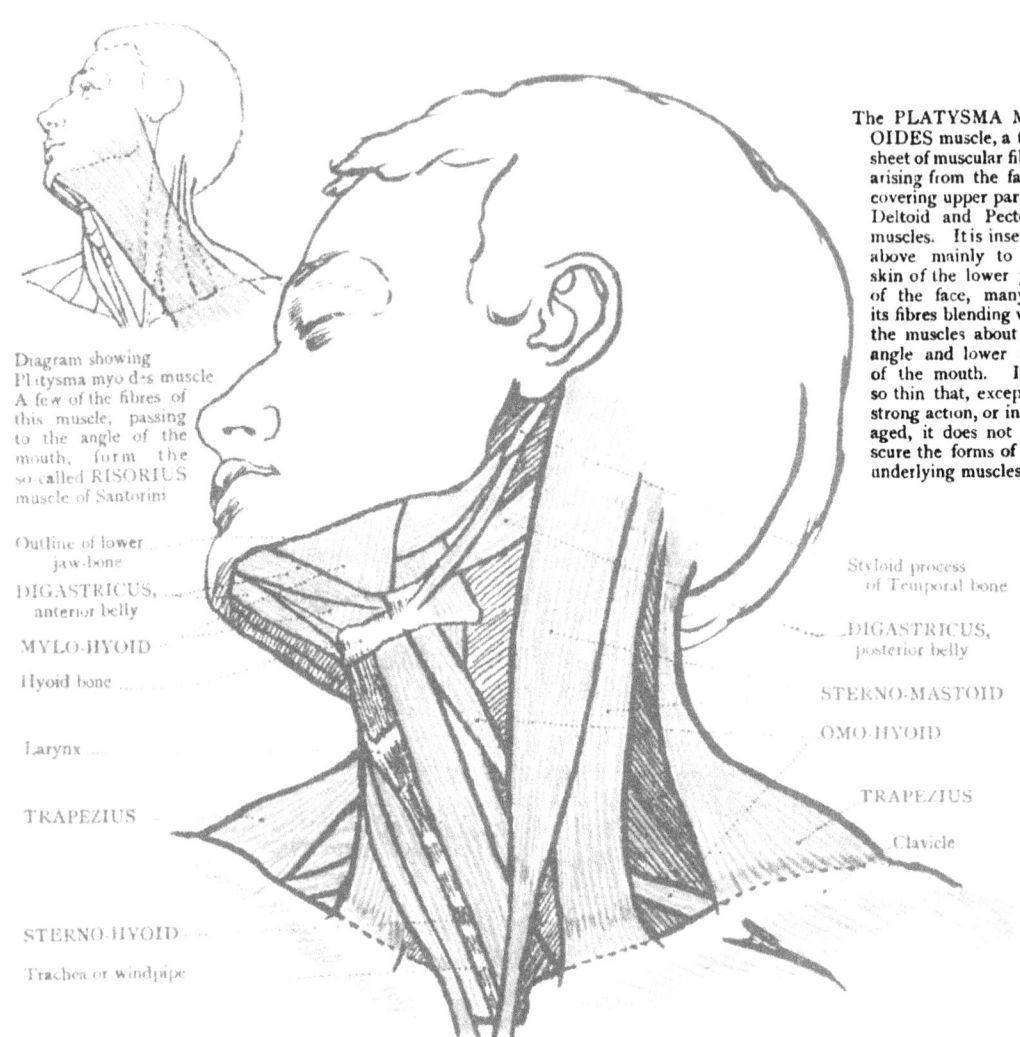

The PLATYSMA M
OIDES muscle, a th
sheet of muscular fibr
arising from the fasc
covering upper part
Deltoid and Pector
muscles. It is insert
above mainly to t
skin of the lower p
of the face, many
its fibres blending wi
the muscles about t
angle and lower p
of the mouth. It
so thin that, except
strong action, or in t
aged, it does not o
scure the forms of t
underlying muscles

Diagram showing
Platysma myo d-s muscle
A few of the fibres of
this muscle, passing
to the angle of the
mouth, form the
so-called RISORIUS
muscle of Santorini

Outline of lower
jaw-bone

DIGASTRICUS,
anterior belly

MYLO-HYOID

Hyoid bone

Larynx

TRAPEZIUS

STERNO-HYOID

Trachea or windpipe

Styloid process
of Temporal bone

DIGASTRICUS,
posterior belly

STERNO-MASTOID

OMO-HYOID

TRAPEZIUS

Clavicle

The STERNO-MASTOID muscle arises by two heads from the Sternum and Clavicle; it is inserted into the mastoid process of the Temporal bone and to the superior curved line of the Occipital bone. The sternal origin is in the form of a rounded tendon; it is separated by an interval from the clavicular origin which is composed of fleshy and aponeurotic fibres

The STERNO-HYOID muscle arises from the Clavicle and Sternum and is inserted into the Hyoid bone

The OMO-HYOID muscle passes from the upper border of the Scapula to the Hyoid bone. It consists of two fleshy bellies united by a central tendon, which is held in position by fascia attached to the Cartilage of the 1st Rib and to Sternum

The DIGASTRICUS muscle consists of two fleshy bellies united by an intermediate, rounded tendon, held in connection with the side of the Hyoid bone by a fibrous loop. The posterior belly arises from the mastoid process of the Temporal bone; the anterior belly arise from the lower jaw-bone

42

# MUSCLES OF THE TRUNK.

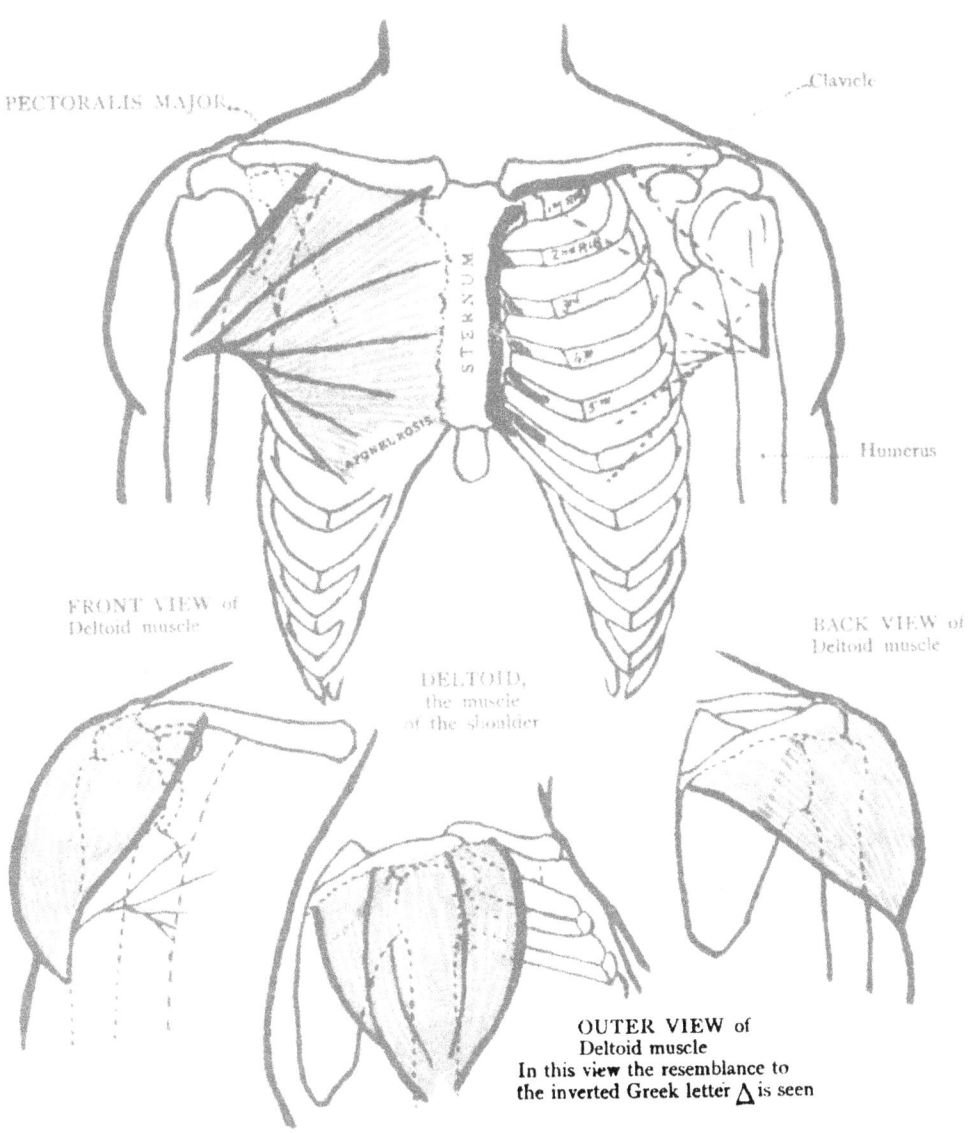

PECTORALIS MAJOR

Clavicle

STERNUM

1st RIB
2nd RIB
3rd
4th
5th

APONEUROSIS

Humerus

FRONT VIEW of
Deltoid muscle

BACK VIEW of
Deltoid muscle

DELTOID,
the muscle
of the shoulder

OUTER VIEW of
Deltoid muscle
In this view the resemblance to
the inverted Greek letter $\Delta$ is seen

The PECTORALIS MAJOR muscle
  arises from the
  Clavicle, inner third,
  Sternum,
  Cartilages of ribs, 2nd to 6th,
  and from the
  Aponeurosis of the External oblique muscle
    It is inserted into the
  Humerus, at the outer lip of the bicipital
groove

The DELTOID muscle
  arises from the
  Scapula, spine and acromion process,
  Clavicle, outer third,
    and is inserted into the
  Humerus at the V-shaped deltoid
impression

43

# MUSCLES OF THE TRUNK.

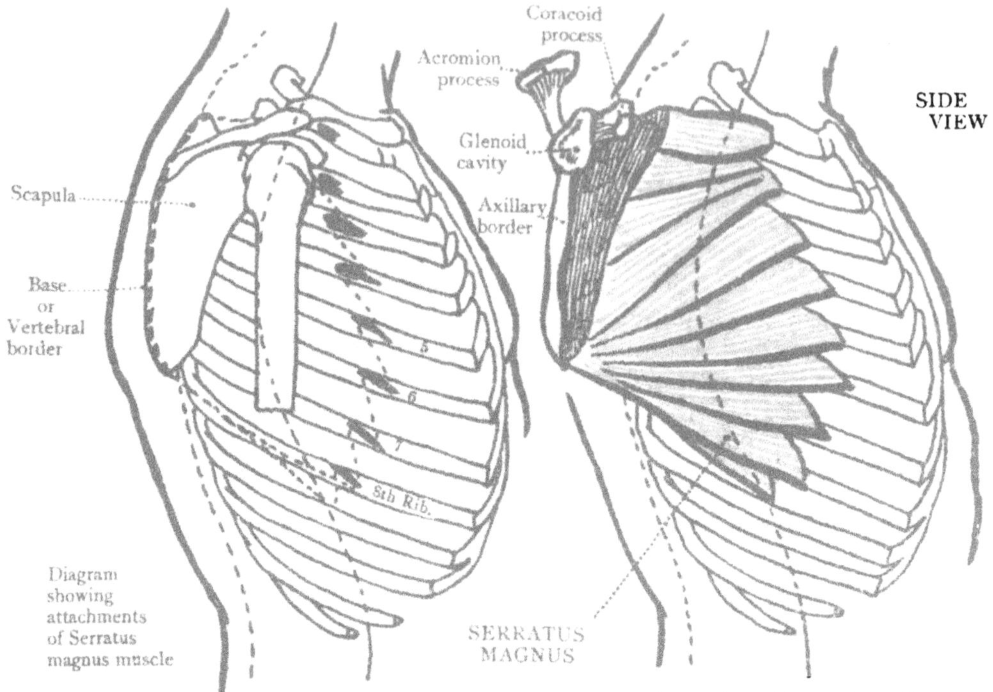

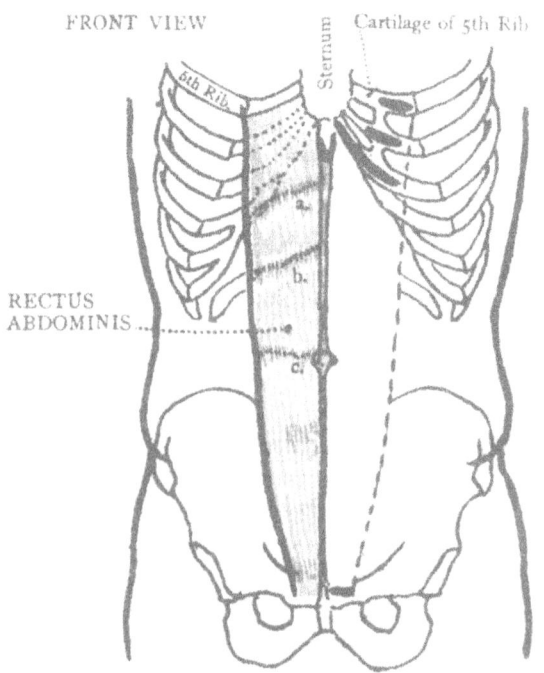

SIDE VIEW

Coracoid process

Acromion process

Glenoid cavity

Axillary border

Scapula

Base or Vertebral border

5
6
7
8th Rib.

Diagram showing attachments of Serratus magnus muscle

SERRATUS MAGNUS

FRONT VIEW

Sternum

Cartilage of 5th Rib

6th Rib

a.

b.

c.

RECTUS ABDOMINIS

In the above diagram the axillary border of the Scapula is moved away from the side of the trunk to show the complete muscle

The SERRATUS MAGNUS muscle arises from the upper 8 Ribs and the intervening Costal fascia,
and is inserted into the base or vertebral border of the Scapula
The muscle lies between the Scapula and the ribs

NOTE—
The serrated markings of the superficial part of this muscle lie in a curved line, with convexity downwards, which being continued would pass through the nipple

The RECTUS ABDOMINIS is attached above to the Cartilages of the 5th, 6th, and 7th Ribs, and to the tip of the Sternum
It is attached below to the Pelvis at the Pubic crest and Pubic symphysis
The tendinous intersections of the Rectus are marked on the diagram a. b. c.

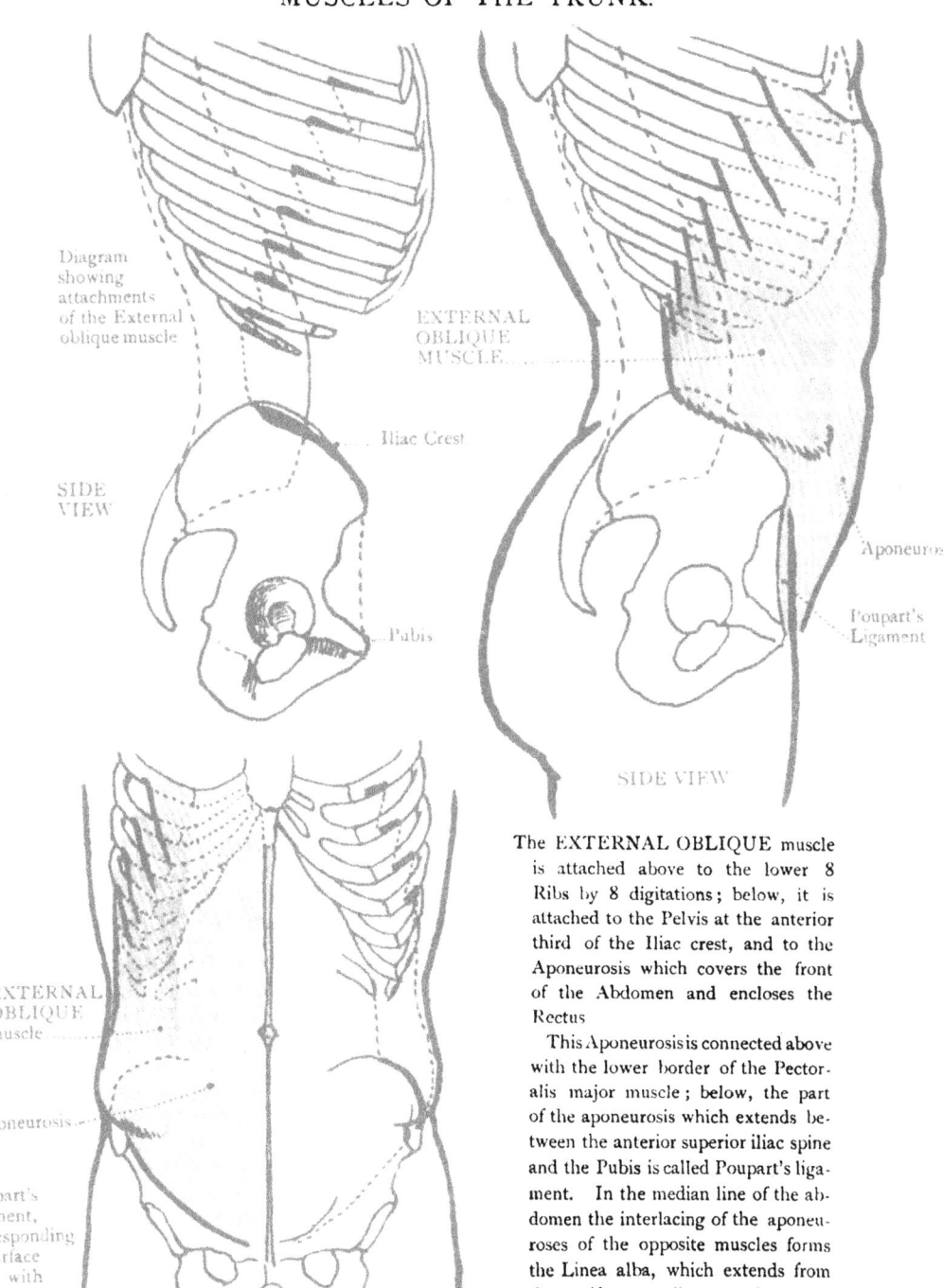

Diagram
showing
attachments
of the External
oblique muscle

EXTERNAL
OBLIQUE
MUSCLE

Iliac Crest

SIDE
VIEW

Pubis

Aponeurosis

Poupart's
Ligament

SIDE VIEW

EXTERNAL
OBLIQUE
muscle

Aponeurosis

Poupart's
ligament,
corresponding
on surface
orm with
he Fold of
he Groin

FRONT VIEW

The EXTERNAL OBLIQUE muscle is attached above to the lower 8 Ribs by 8 digitations; below, it is attached to the Pelvis at the anterior third of the Iliac crest, and to the Aponeurosis which covers the front of the Abdomen and encloses the Rectus

This Aponeurosis is connected above with the lower border of the Pectoralis major muscle; below, the part of the aponeurosis which extends between the anterior superior iliac spine and the Pubis is called Poupart's ligament. In the median line of the abdomen the interlacing of the aponeuroses of the opposite muscles forms the Linea alba, which extends from the ensiform cartilage or tip of the Sternum to the Pubis

# MUSCLES OF THE TRUNK.

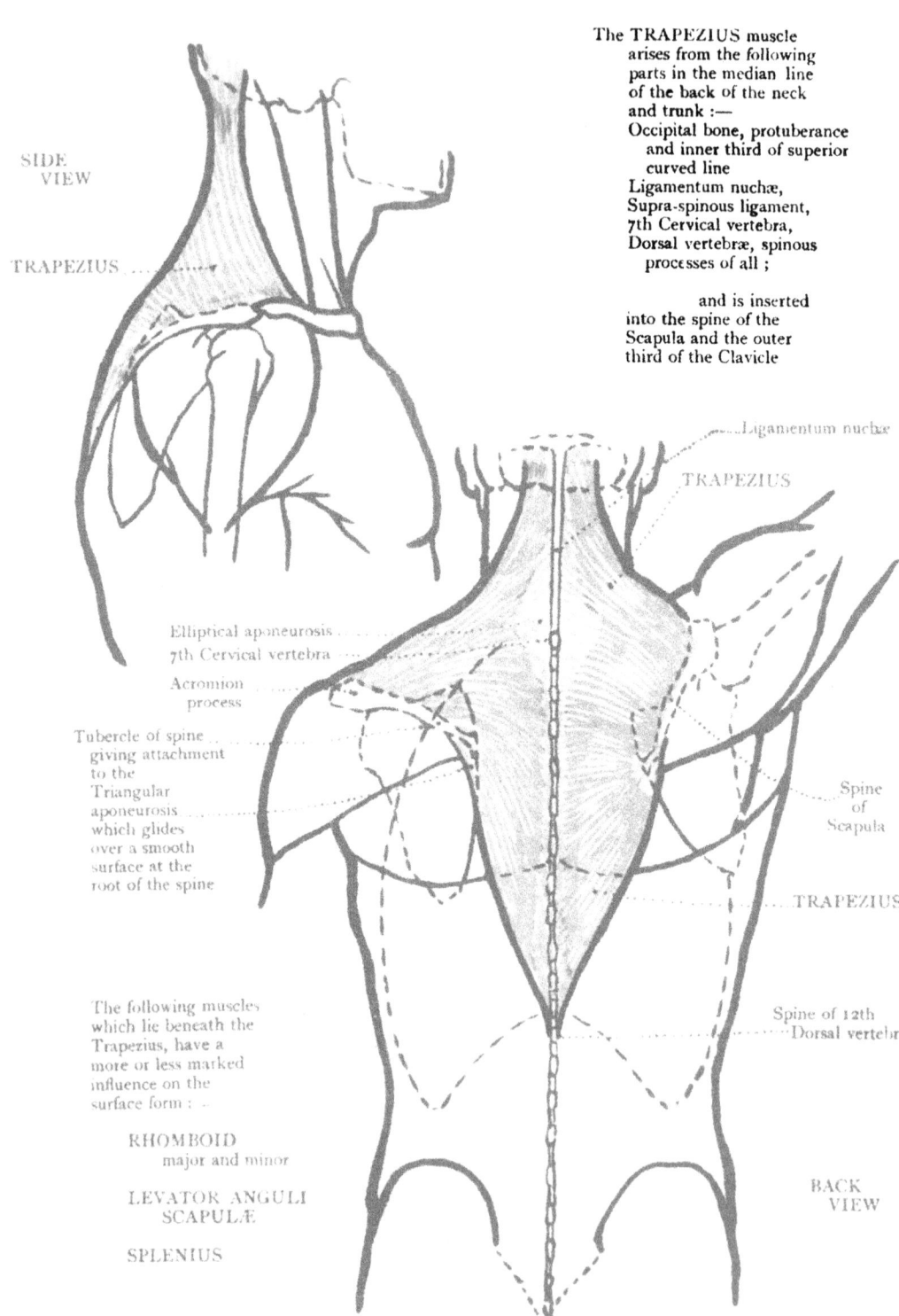

SIDE
VIEW

TRAPEZIUS

The **TRAPEZIUS** muscle
arises from the following
parts in the median line
of the back of the neck
and trunk :—
Occipital bone, protuberance
and inner third of superior
curved line
Ligamentum nuchæ,
Supra-spinous ligament,
7th Cervical vertebra,
Dorsal vertebræ, spinous
processes of all ;

and is inserted
into the spine of the
Scapula and the outer
third of the Clavicle

Ligamentum nuchæ

TRAPEZIUS

Elliptical aponeurosis
7th Cervical vertebra

Acromion
process

Tubercle of spine
giving attachment
to the
Triangular
aponeurosis
which glides
over a smooth
surface at the
root of the spine

Spine
of
Scapula

TRAPEZIUS

The following muscles
which lie beneath the
Trapezius, have a
more or less marked
influence on the
surface form : —

Spine of 12th
Dorsal vertebra

RHOMBOID
major and minor

LEVATOR ANGULI
SCAPULÆ

SPLENIUS

BACK
VIEW

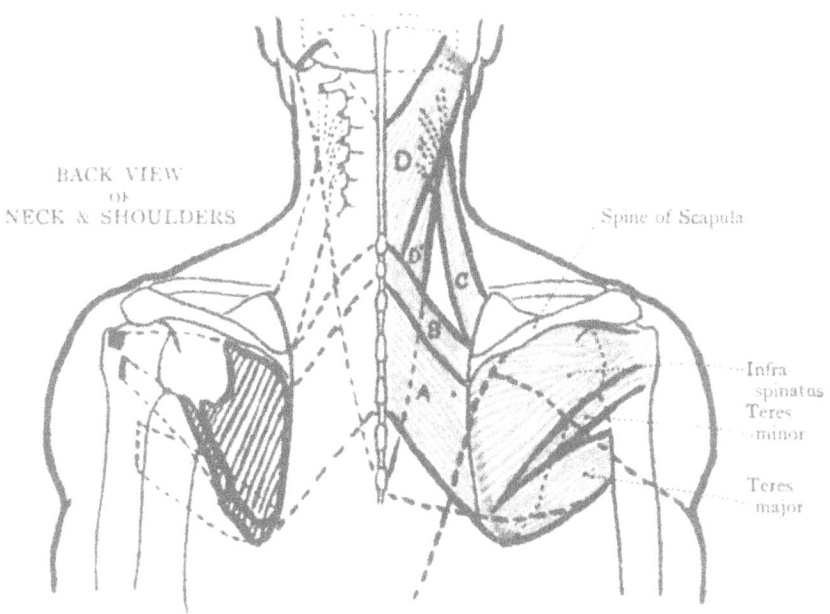

BACK VIEW
OF
NECK & SHOULDERS

Spine of Scapula

Infra-
spinatus
Teres
minor

Teres
major

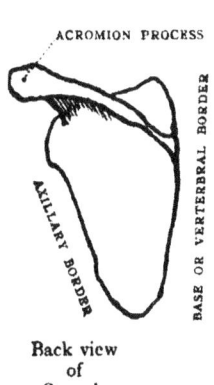

ACROMION PROCESS

BASE OR VERTEBRAL BORDER

AXILLARY BORDER

Back view
of
Scapula

Muscles covered by Trapezius

A.—RHOMBOIDEUS MAJOR  } arise
B.—        ,,        MINOR  }
from the spines of the vertebræ,
7th Cervical to 4th or 5th Dorsal,
and are inserted into the
base of the Scapula.

C.—LEVATOR ANGULI SCAPULÆ
arises from the transverse processes
of the upper 4 Cervical vertebræ
and is inserted into the upper
part of the base of the Scapula.

D. }
D' }  SPLENIUS arises from the
ligamentum nuchae and from
the spines of the vertebræ,
7th Cervical and 6 upper Dorsal.
It divides into the Splenius Capitis (D),
inserted into mastoid process of
Temporal bone, and Splenius Colii (D')
inserted into transverse processes
of 2 or 3 upper Cervical vertebræ.

Muscles which are superficial in the
triangular interval bounded by the
Trapezius, Deltoid, and Latissimus Dorsi.

INFRA-SPINATUS arises from the back of the Scapula and
from the strong fascia which covers the
muscle.   It is inserted into the back of the
great tuberosity of the Humerus, uniting its
tendon with that of the Teres minor.

TERES MINOR arises from the back of the Scapula at its
axillary border and is inserted into the
Humerus immediately below the Infra-spinatus tendon.

TERES MAJOR arises from the back of the inferior angle of
the Scapula and, passing to the front of the
Humerus, is inserted into the inner lip of the
bicipital groove.

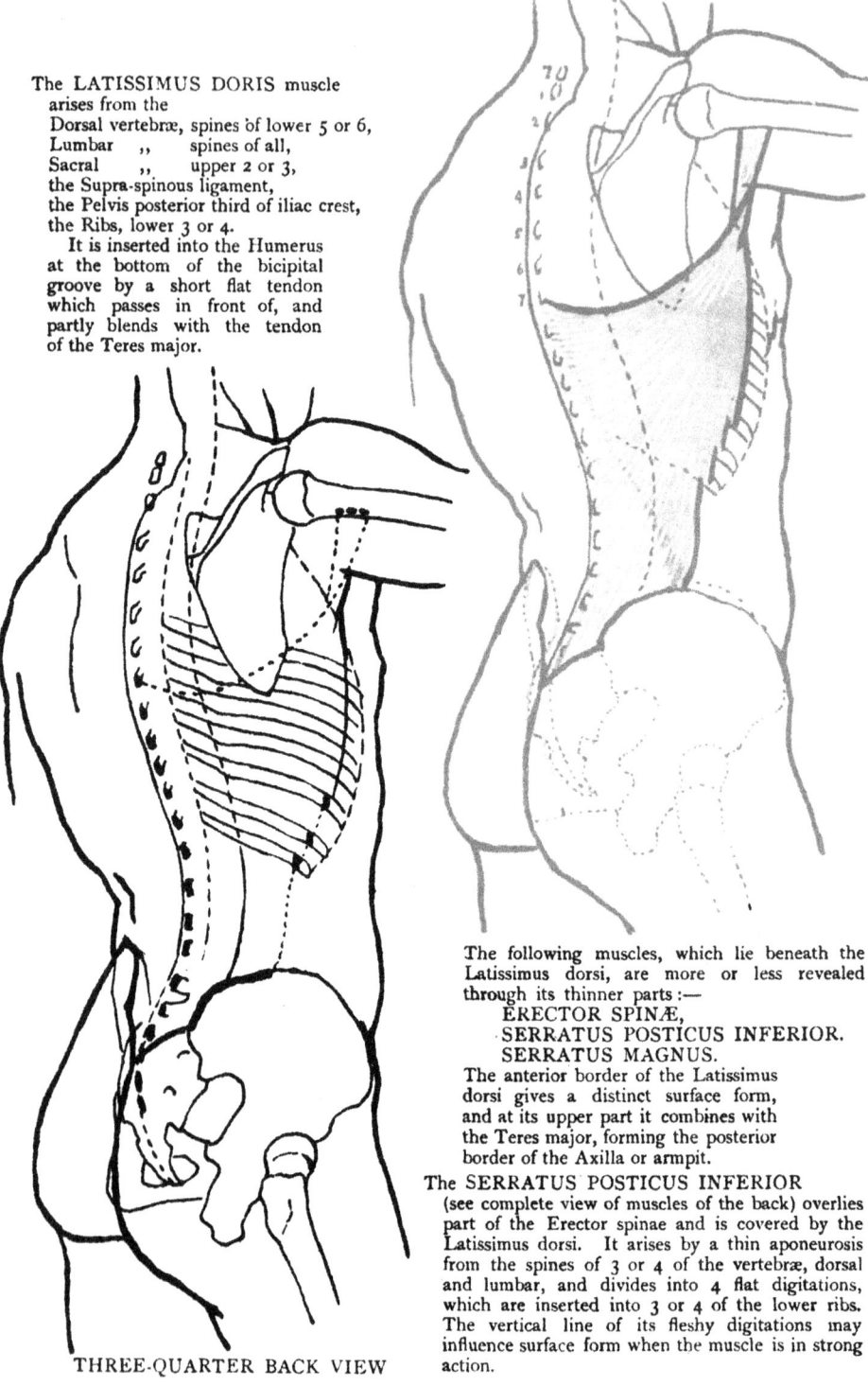

The LATISSIMUS DORIS muscle arises from the
Dorsal vertebræ, spines of lower 5 or 6,
Lumbar ,, spines of all,
Sacral ,, upper 2 or 3,
the Supra-spinous ligament,
the Pelvis posterior third of iliac crest,
the Ribs, lower 3 or 4.

It is inserted into the Humerus at the bottom of the bicipital groove by a short flat tendon which passes in front of, and partly blends with the tendon of the Teres major.

The following muscles, which lie beneath the Latissimus dorsi, are more or less revealed through its thinner parts :—
　　ERECTOR SPINÆ,
　　SERRATUS POSTICUS INFERIOR.
　　SERRATUS MAGNUS.
The anterior border of the Latissimus dorsi gives a distinct surface form, and at its upper part it combines with the Teres major, forming the posterior border of the Axilla or armpit.

The SERRATUS POSTICUS INFERIOR (see complete view of muscles of the back) overlies part of the Erector spinae and is covered by the Latissimus dorsi. It arises by a thin aponeurosis from the spines of 3 or 4 of the vertebræ, dorsal and lumbar, and divides into 4 flat digitations, which are inserted into 3 or 4 of the lower ribs. The vertical line of its fleshy digitations may influence surface form when the muscle is in strong action.

THREE-QUARTER BACK VIEW

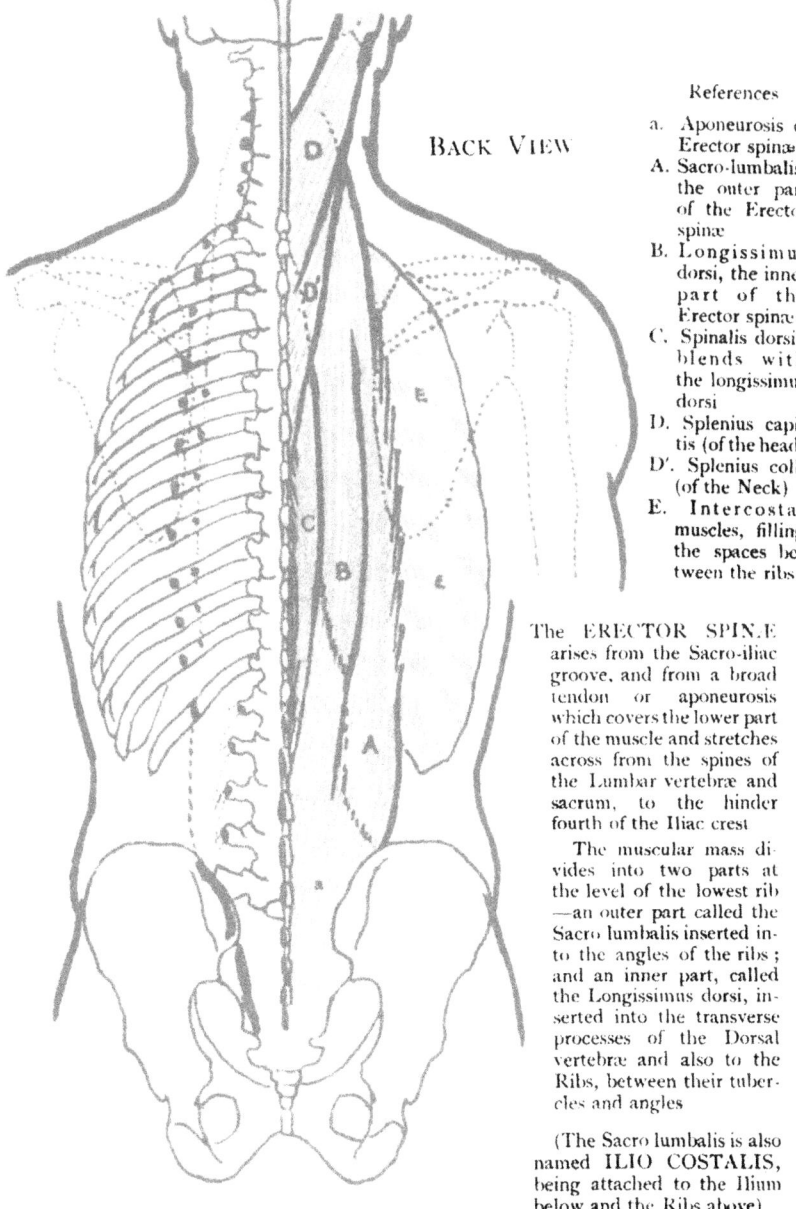

BACK VIEW

## References

a. Aponeurosis of Erector spinæ
A. Sacro-lumbalis, the outer part of the Erector spinæ
B. Longissimus dorsi, the inner part of the Erector spinæ
C. Spinalis dorsi; blends with the longissimus dorsi
D. Splenius capitis (of the head)
D'. Splenius colli (of the Neck)
E. Intercostal muscles, filling the spaces between the ribs

The ERECTOR SPINÆ arises from the Sacro-iliac groove, and from a broad tendon or aponeurosis which covers the lower part of the muscle and stretches across from the spines of the Lumbar vertebræ and sacrum, to the hinder fourth of the Iliac crest

The muscular mass divides into two parts at the level of the lowest rib —an outer part called the Sacro lumbalis inserted into the angles of the ribs; and an inner part, called the Longissimus dorsi, inserted into the transverse processes of the Dorsal vertebræ and also to the Ribs, between their tubercles and angles

(The Sacro lumbalis is also named ILIO COSTALIS, being attached to the Ilium below and the Ribs above)

The Erector spinæ muscles, with their complicated accessory muscles and prolongations into the neck, fill in the grooves seen in an articulated skeleton, between the spines of the vertebræ and the angles of the ribs on either side. Although covered by the superficial muscles, these fleshy columns have a decided influence on the surface form, more especially in the lumbar region of the back.

# MUSCLES OF THE THIGH—FRONT VIEW.

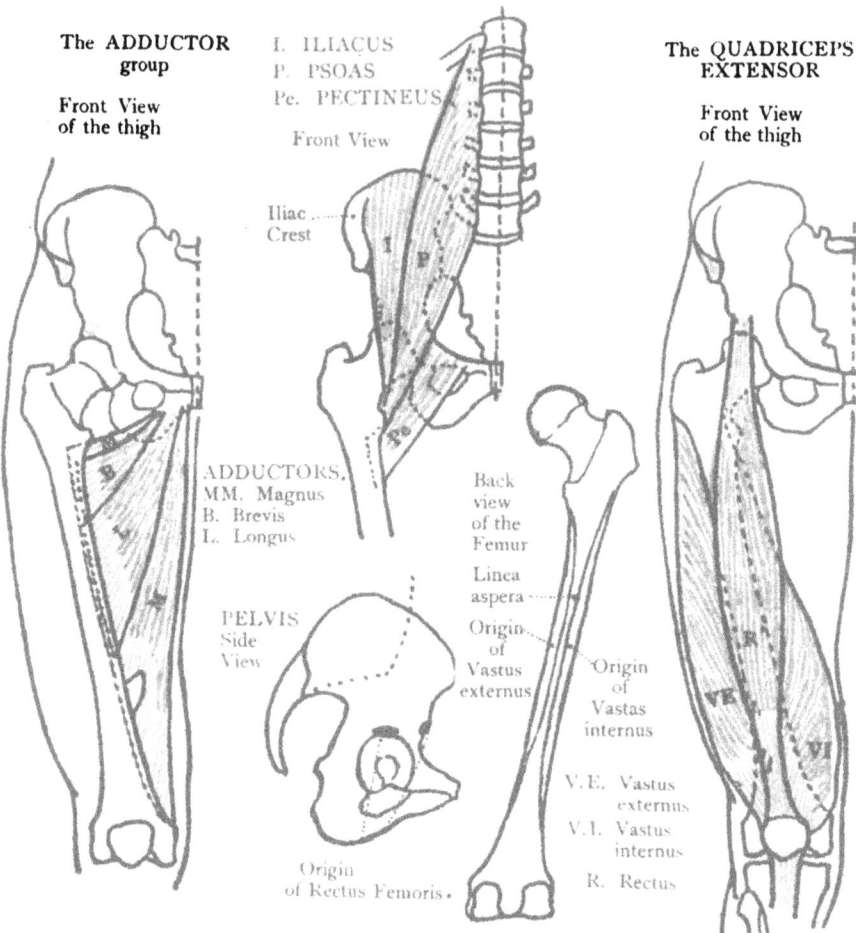

The ADDUCTOR group

Front View of the thigh

I. ILIACUS
P. PSOAS
Pe. PECTINEUS

Front View

The QUADRICEPS EXTENSOR

Front View of the thigh

Iliac Crest

ADDUCTORS.
MM. Magnus
B. Brevis
L. Longus

PELVIS
Side View

Origin of Rectus Femoris.

Back view of the Femur

Linea aspera

Origin of Vastus externus

Origin of Vastus internus

V.E. Vastus externus

V.I. Vastus internus

R. Rectus

## Flexors of the THIGH on the body

The ILIACUS, and PSOAS, } from the Pelvis at the iliac crest and iliac fossa; from the vertebræ are inserted together into the lesser trochanter of the Femur

## Adductors of the THIGH

The PECTINEUS, from the Pelvis, at the ilio-pectineal line, to the back of the Femur

The ADDUCTOR LONGUS from the Pubic portion of the Pelvis to the linea aspera, or rough line, on the back of the Femur

The ADDUCTOR MAGNUS from the Pubis and Ischium it is inserted into the whole length of the linea aspera. The internal portion of the muscle terminates in a tendon attached to the Adductor tubercle on the inner condyle of the Femur

## The QUADRICEPS EXTENSOR

The RECTUS FEMORIS arises by two tendons from the Pelvis, at the Anterior inferior iliac spine, and from a groove over the acetabulum

The VASTUS EXTERNUS arises from the Femur at the great trochanter and along the outer lip of the linea aspera, or rough line, on the back of the Femur

The VASTAS INTERNUS and CRUREUS (deep seated, being covered by the Rectus) } from the inner lip of linea aspera and from almost the whole length of front and inner side of shaft of Femur

These four muscles are, together, called the Quadriceps extensor. Their tendons uniting below, are inserted into the Patella, and are continued by the ligamentum patellæ to be ultimately attached to the tubercle of the Tibia

The Patella may be regarded as a sesamoid bone developed in the tendon of the Quadriceps extensor. Note that the fleshy fibres of the Vastus internus descend lower than those of the Vastus externus

SARTORIUS
and
GRACILIS

Diagram of
muscles on
front of thigh

Mnemonic of the
arrangement of muscles
on front of thigh, the
cross line of the letter N
representing the Sartorius

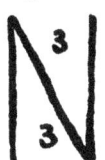

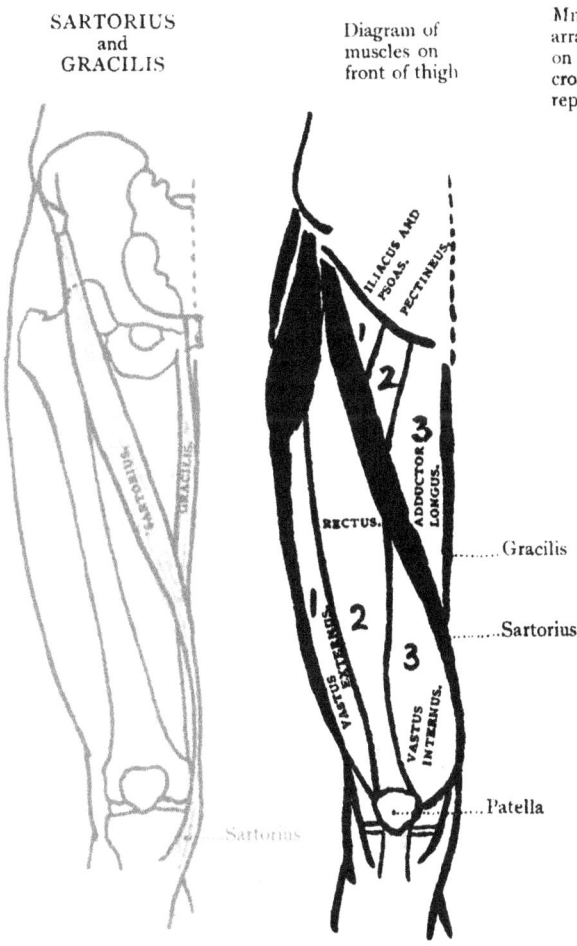

Diagram of front view
of lower limb with
suggested lines of
construction

........Gracilis

........Sartorius

........Patella

The SARTORIUS muscle arises
from the anterior superior iliac
spine, and is inserted by an aponeurosis into the upper part of the
inner surface of the Tibia

The GRACILIS arises from the
margin of the Pubic symphysis,
and descending ramus of the Pubis.
It tapers down to a long tendon
which passes close behind the
Sartorius, to be inserted into the
Tibia

NOTE.—The blending of the line of
the Sartorius muscle with the subcutaneous surface of the Tibia
forms an important running line
in drawing the front view of the
leg

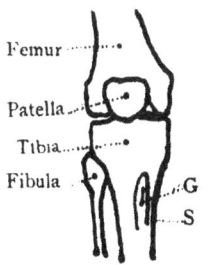

Femur
Patella
Tibia
Fibula
G
S

S. Insertion of Sartorius
G.    ,,    ,, Gracilis

# MUSCLES OF THE BUTTOCK AND HIP.

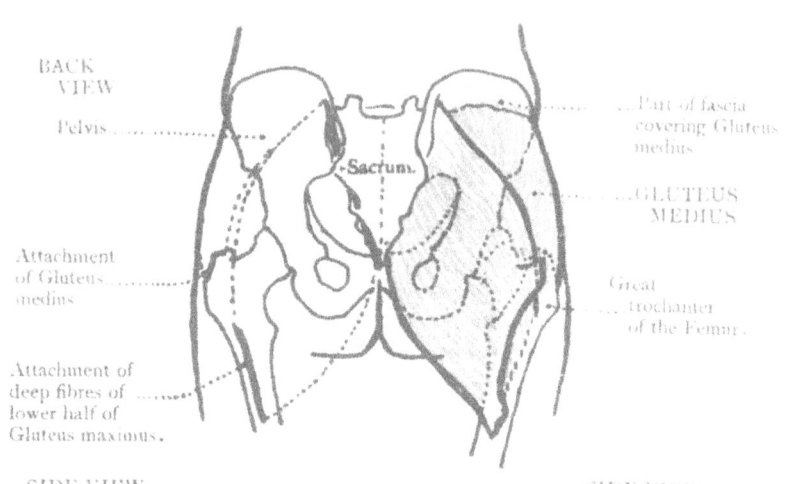

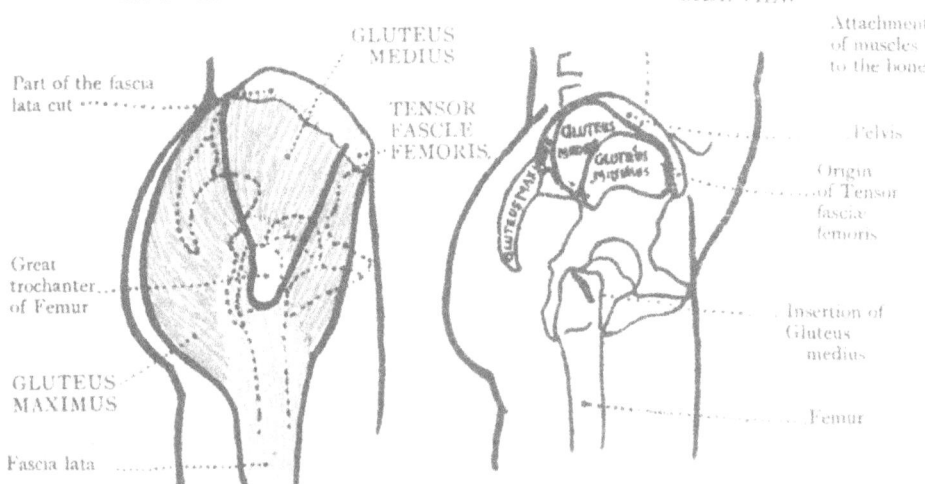

The **GLUTEUS MAXIMUS** muscle arises from the posterior fourth of the iliac crest, from the Sacrum and Coccyx, from the aponeurosis of the Erector spinæ muscle, and from the great Sacro-sciatic ligament. The deeper fibres of the lower half of the muscle are inserted into the linea aspera on the back of the Femur; the fibres of the upper half and the superficial fibres of the lower portion, terminate in a strong tendinous lamina which passes across the great trochanter and is inserted into the fascia lata of the thigh

The GLUTEUS MEDIUS muscle (partly covered by the G. maximus; and its superficial portion lying between G. maximus and the Tensor fasciæ femoris, covered by a strong fascia) arises from the iliac crest and part of the outer surface of the Ilium. It converges to a strong flattened tendon, which is inserted into the great trochanter of the Femur

The **TENSOR VAGINÆ** or **FASCIÆ FEMORIS** arises from the iliac crest close to the antr. supr. iliac spine. It is inserted into the fascia lata

# MUSCLES OF THE THIGH—BACK VIEW.

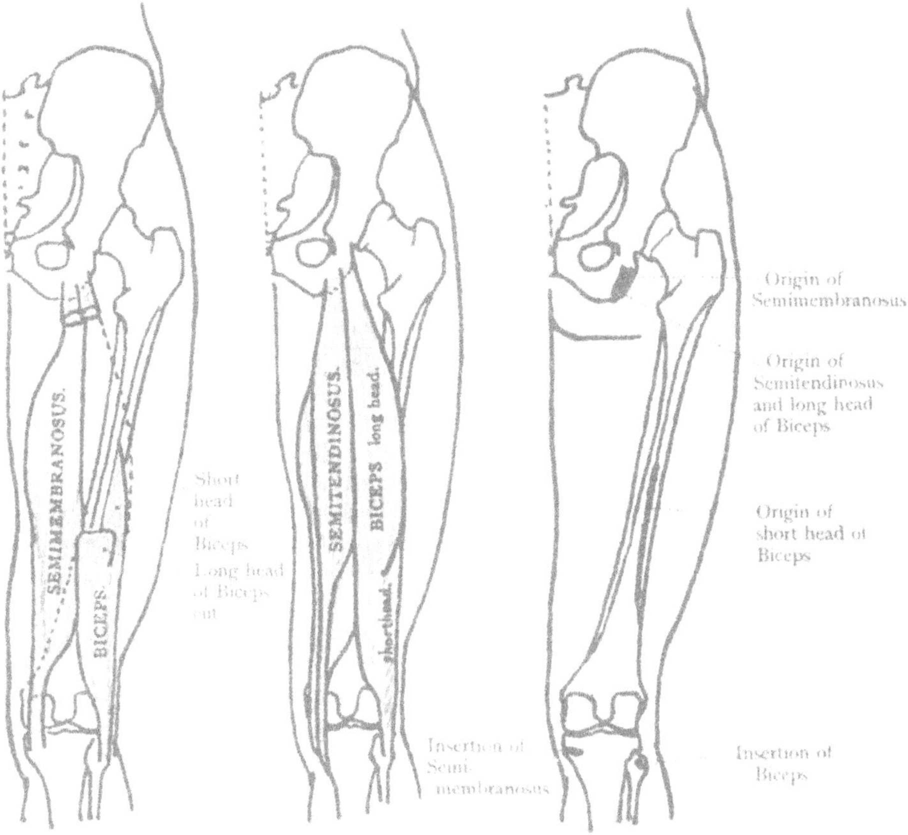

Origin of
Semimembranosus

Origin of
Semitendinosus
and long head
of Biceps

Origin of
short head of
Biceps

Insertion of
Biceps

SEMIMEMBRANOSUS.

BICEPS.

Short
head
of
Biceps

Long head
of Biceps
cut

SEMITENDINOSUS.

BICEPS long head.

short head.

Insertion of
Semi-
membranosus

The HAMSTRING muscles,
flexors of the leg

The BICEPS (the outer hamstring) arises by two heads
the long head from the back of the tuberosity of the
Ischium by a tendon common to it and the Semitendinosus ; the short head from part of the linea aspera
on the back of the Femur. It is inserted into the
head of the Fibula with an expansion of the tendon
to the Tibia.

The SEMITENDINOSUS (together with the semimembranosus forming the inner hamstring), arises from
the tuberosity of the Ischium. It tapers below to a
very long tendon inserted into the upper part of the
inner surface of the Tibia.

The SEMIMEMBRANOSUS (so named from the mem-
branous expansion on its anterior and posterior sur-
faces) arises from the tuberosity of the Ischium and
is inserted into the back of the inner tuberosity of
the Tibia.

Front View of the bones
at the knee

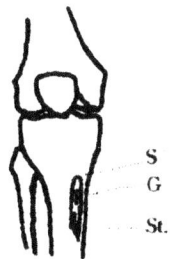

S
G
St.

St. Insertion of
Semitendinosus
G Insertion of Gracilis
S ,, ,, Sartorius

Muscles of the calf
of the leg

The GASTROCNEMIUS muscle arises by two heads from the Femur immediately above the condyles, and ends below in a broad tendon which joins with that of the Soleus to form the Tendo-Achillis. Each tendon of origin spreads out into an apo-neurosis from which some of the muscular fibres arise. The two heads meet in the median line of the calf

The SOLEUS, a broad flat muscle, shaped like a sole-fish, arises from the back of the Tibia and Fibula. The fleshy fibres are short and pass backward to an aponeurosis which joins below with the tendon of the Gastrocnemius, forming the Tendo-Achillis, which is inserted into the Os calcis or heel-bone

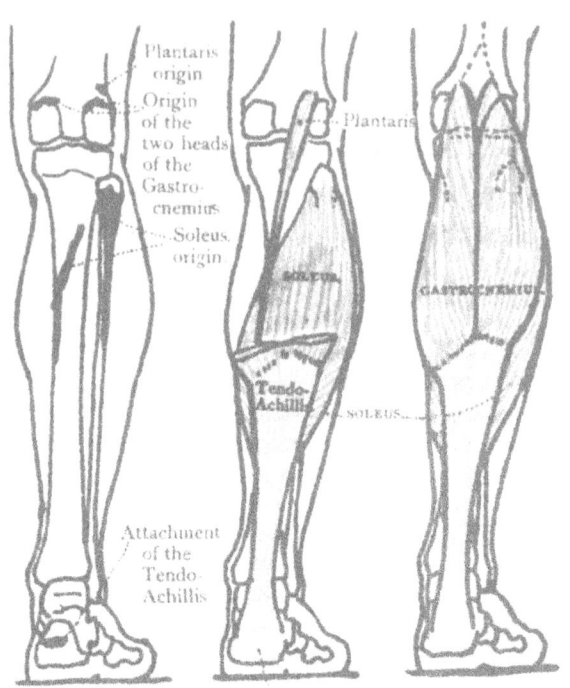

Deep muscles of the back of the leg. These muscles are superficial only at the lower part of the inner border of the leg. They arise from the back of the Tibia and Fibula and from the interosseous membrane, which extends between these two bones and separates the muscles of the front from those on the back of the leg.

The FLEXOR LONGUS DIGITORUM terminates below in a tendon which de-scends behind the inner malleolus along with the T. posticus, and crossing super-ficially to the tendon of the Flexor longus pollicis, passes into the sole of the foot and divides into four tendons for the outer toes.

The TIBIALIS POSTICUS is inserted into the Scaphoid bone, with prolonga-tions to most of the tarsal and metatarsal bones

The FLEXOR LONGUS POLLICIS or HALLUCIS, almost entirely hidden, is inserted into the base of the last phalanx of the great toe

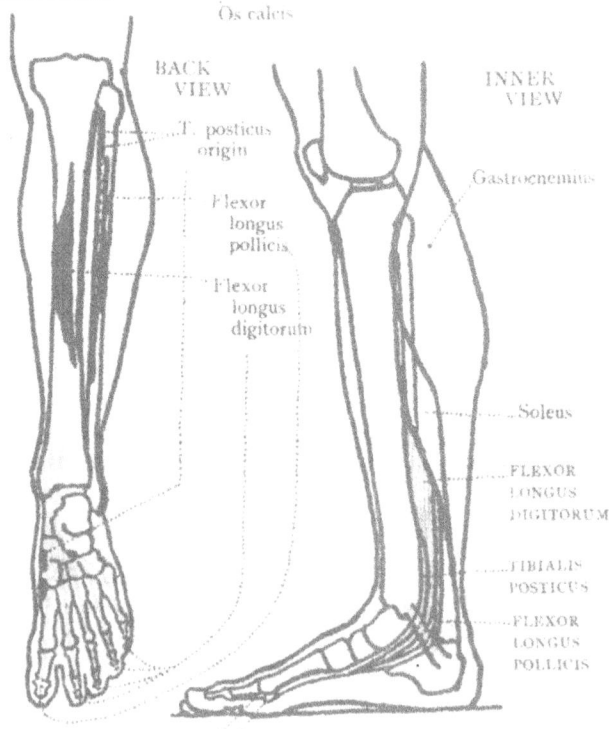

54

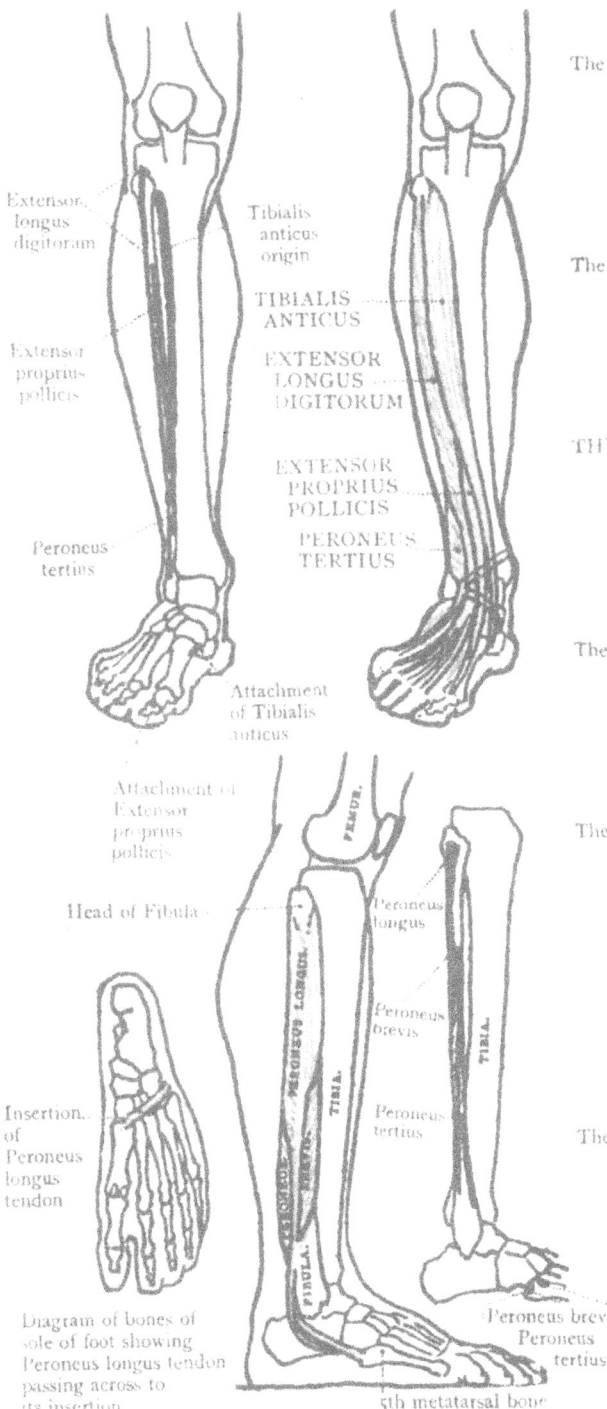

Extensor longus digitorum

Tibialis anticus origin

Extensor proprius pollicis

TIBIALIS ANTICUS

EXTENSOR LONGUS DIGITORUM

EXTENSOR PROPRIUS POLLICIS

PERONEUS TERTIUS

Peroneus tertius

Attachment of Tibialis anticus

Attachment of Extensor proprius pollicis

Head of Fibula

Peroneus longus

Peroneus brevis

Insertion of Peroneus longus tendon

Peroneus tertius

Diagram of bones of sole of foot showing Peroneus longus tendon passing across to its insertion

Peroneus brevis

Peroneus tertius

5th metatarsal bone

OUTER VIEW

The **TIBIALIS ANTICUS** arises from the Tibia at its outer tuberosity and outer surface of the shaft, and from the interosseous membrane. Its tendon, after passing through the innermost compartment of the anterior annular ligament, is inserted into the inner cuneiform bone and the base of the metatarsal bone of the great toe

The **EXTENSOR PROPRIUS POLLICIS** or **HALLUCIS** (of the great toe) arises from the front of the Fibula and the interosseous membrane. Its tendon, passing through a compartment of the annular ligament, is inserted into the base of the last phalanx of the great toe

THE **EXTENSOR LONGUS DIGITORUM** arises from the outer tuberosity of the Tibia and the upper three-fourths of the shaft of the Fibula, and from the interosseous membrane. Its tendon passing through the annular ligament divides into four slips which are inserted into the four outer toes at their 2nd and 3rd phalanges

The **PERONEUS TERTIUS** is a part of the Ex. longus digitorum. It arises from the lower fourth of the shaft of the Fibula. The tendon, after passing through the same compartment of the annular ligament as the Ex. longus, is inserted into the base of the metatarsal bone of the little toe

The **PERONEUS LONGUS** arises from the head and upper two-thirds of outer surface of the shaft of the Fibula. It terminates in a long tendon, which, passing behind and beneath the outer malleolus in a groove common to it and the Peroneus brevis, is directed forwards and downwards to the outer border of the foot and enters a groove on the under surface of the Cuboid bone; it then passes deeply across the sole of the foot to be inserted into the inner cuneiform bone and the base of the metatarsal bone of the great toe.

The **PERONEUS BREVIS** lies beneath the Peroneus longus and arises from the lower two-thirds of the outer surface of the shaft of the Fibula. Its tendon passes behind the outer malleolus along with the Peroneus longus, and separating from the latter at that point, turns forward along the outer side of the foot, to be inserted into the tuberosity of the 5th metatarsal bone

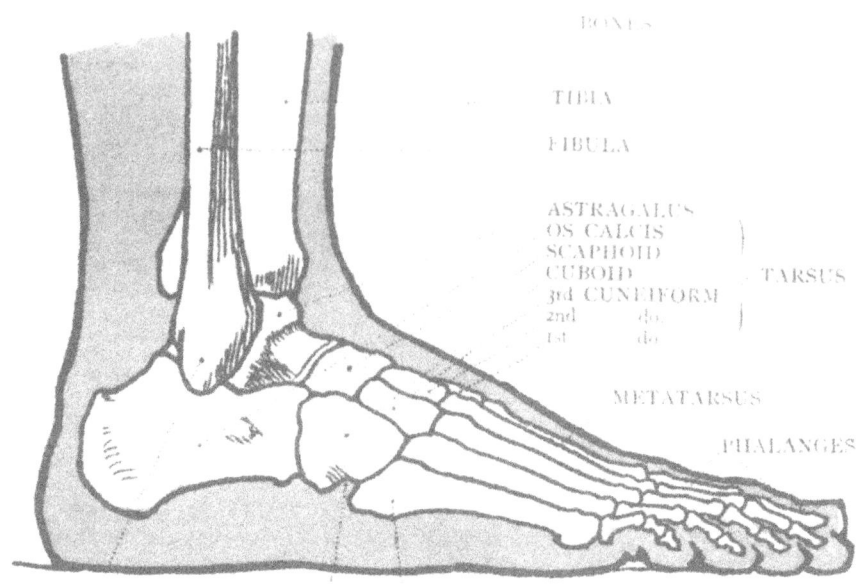

BONES

TIBIA

FIBULA

ASTRAGALUS
OS CALCIS
SCAPHOID
CUBOID                    TARSUS
3rd CUNEIFORM
2nd    do.
1st    do.

METATARSUS

PHALANGES

External malleolus          Tuberosity of 5th Metatarsal bone
of the Fibula               Groove in Cuboid bone for Peroneus longus tendon
(outer ankle)

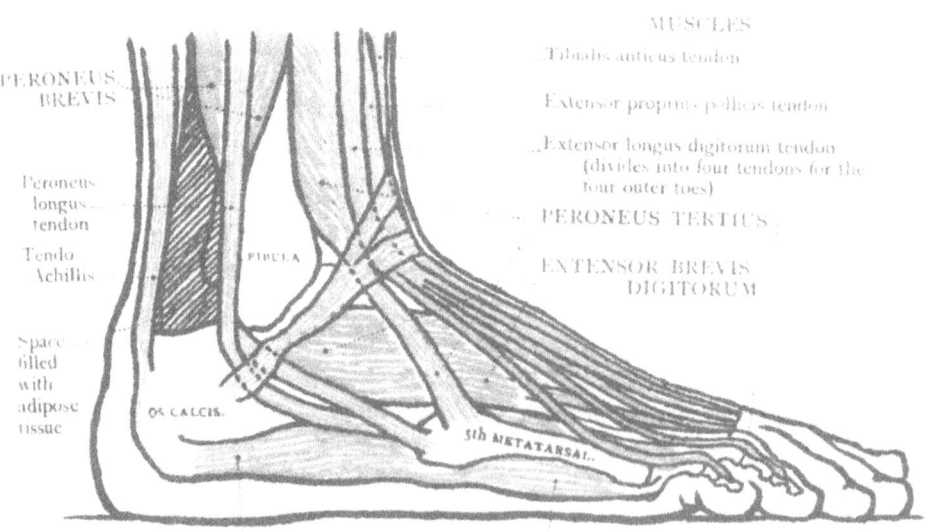

MUSCLES

Tibialis anticus tendon

PERONEUS.         Extensor proprius pollicis tendon
BREVIS
Extensor longus digitorum tendon
(divides into four tendons for the
four outer toes)

Peroneus          PERONEUS TERTIUS
longus
tendon            EXTENSOR BREVIS
Tendo                DIGITORUM
Achillis

Space
filled
with
adipose
tissue      OS CALCIS.

5th METATARSAL.

ABDUCTOR MINIMI DIGITI.

The **ABDUCTOR MINIMI DIGITI** arises from the os calcis and is inserted into the 1st phalanx of the little toe. It is slightly attached in its course to the base of the 5th metatarsal bone

The **EXTENSOR BREVIS DIGITORUM** arises from the os calcis and sends tendons to the four inner toes. This muscle causes an important surface form in front of the outer ankle

# INNER VIEW OF THE FOOT.

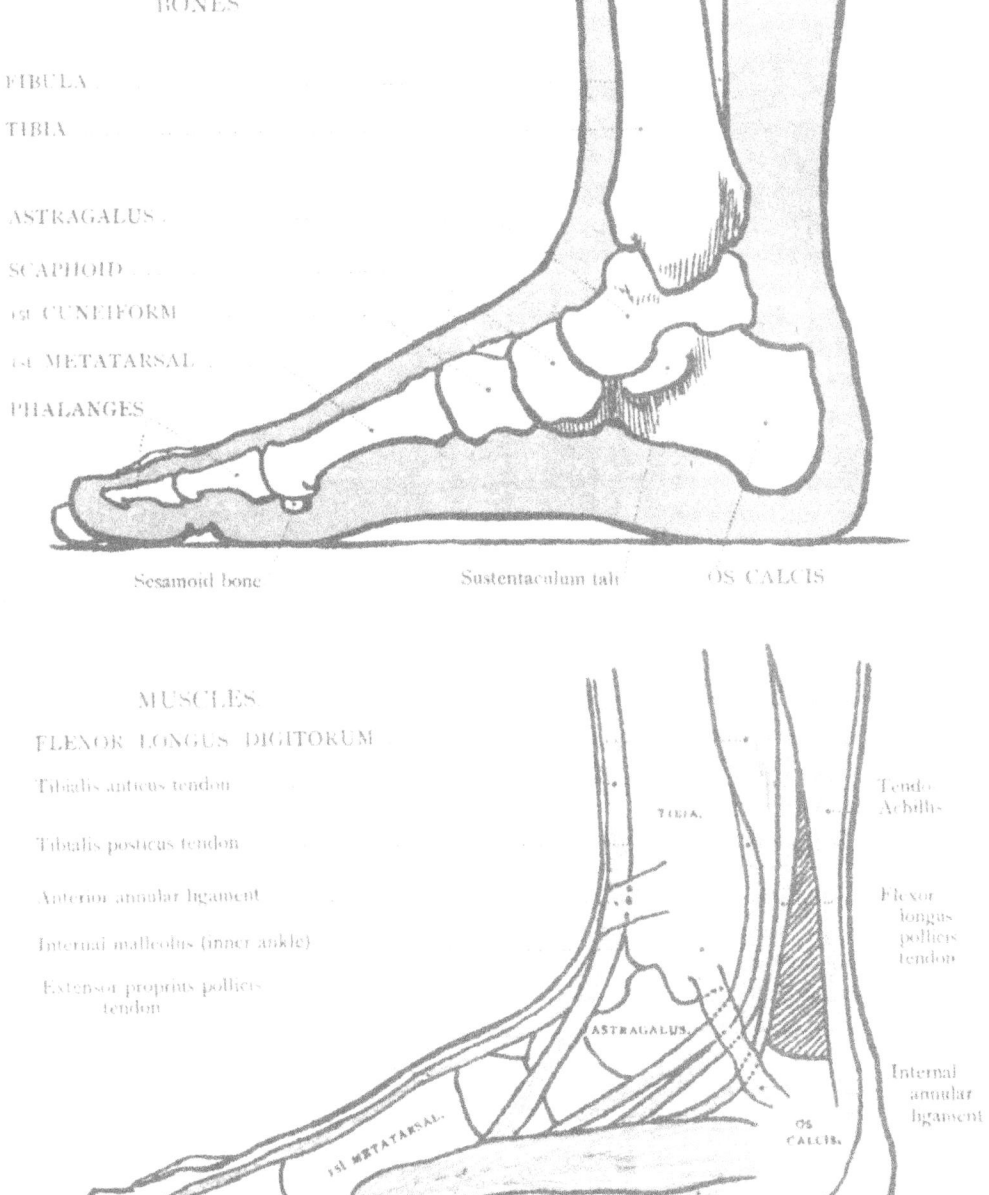

BONES

FIBULA

TIBIA

ASTRAGALUS

SCAPHOID

1st CUNEIFORM

1st METATARSAL

PHALANGES

Sesamoid bone     Sustentaculum tali     OS CALCIS

MUSCLES

FLEXOR LONGUS DIGITORUM

Tibialis anticus tendon

Tibialis posticus tendon

Anterior annular ligament

Internal malleolus (inner ankle)

Extensor proprius pollicis
tendon

TIBIA.

ASTRAGALUS.

1st METATARSAL

OS CALCIS.

Tendo
Achillis

Flexor
longus
pollicis
tendon

Internal
annular
ligament

ABDUCTOR POLLICIS     Plantar fascia

The ABDUCTOR POLLICIS arises from the os calcis and is inserted into the internal sesamoid bone and the 1st phalanx of the great toe.

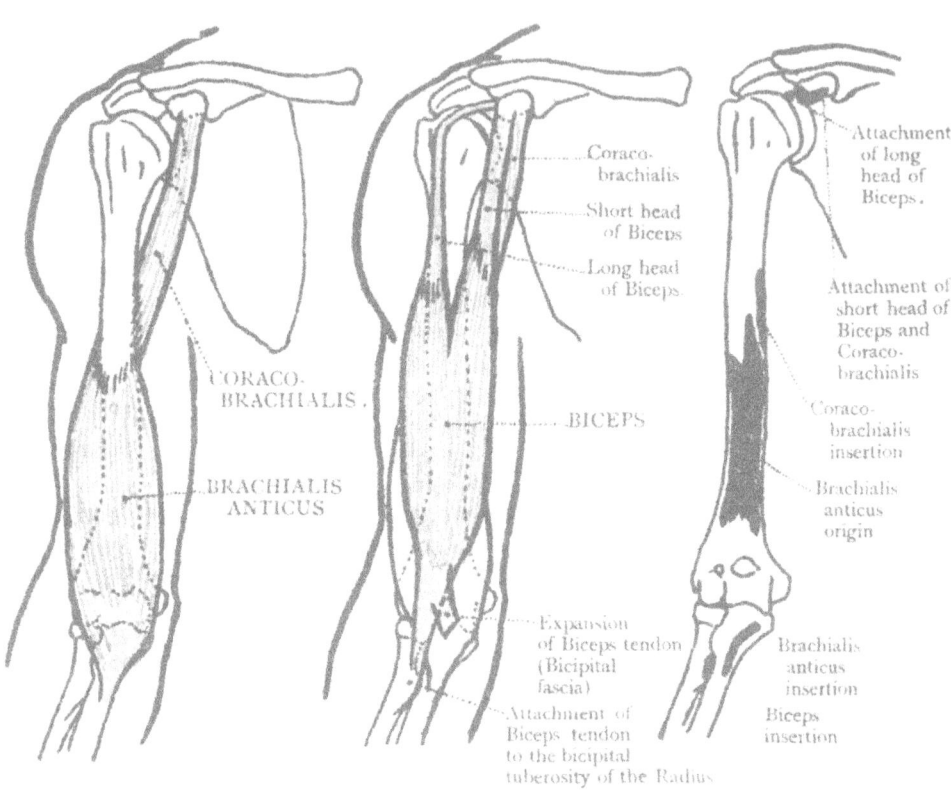

The BICEPS muscle is divided above into two portions or heads. The short head arises from the coracoid process of the Scapula along with the Coraco-brachialis. The long head arises by a long and rounded tendon, from the upper margin of the glenoid cavity of the Scapula, the socket of the shoulder-joint. This tendon passes over the head of the Humerus and lies in the bicipital groove, in which it is held by an expansion of the Pectoralis major tendon. The two portions of the muscle join about the middle of the arm, and the muscular mass terminates above the elbow in a flattened tendon inserted into the back part of the tuberosity of the Radius. Opposite the bend of the elbow the tendon gives off from its inner side, a broad aponeurosis, the Bicipital fascia, which is continuous with the deep fascia or sheath of the muscles of the forearm

The CORACO-BRACHIALIS muscle arises from the coracoid process of the Scapula along with the short head of the Biceps. It is inserted into the Humerus at the middle of the inner surface of the shaft, between the origin of the Triceps and Brachialis Anticus

The BRACHIALIS ANTICUS is a broad muscle which covers the lower half of the front of the Humerus and the front of the elbow joint. It arises from the lower half of the front of the shaft of the Humerus, commencing above at the insertion of the Deltoid, which it embraces by two angular processes. Its fibres converge below to a thick tendon which is inserted into the coronoid process of the Ulna

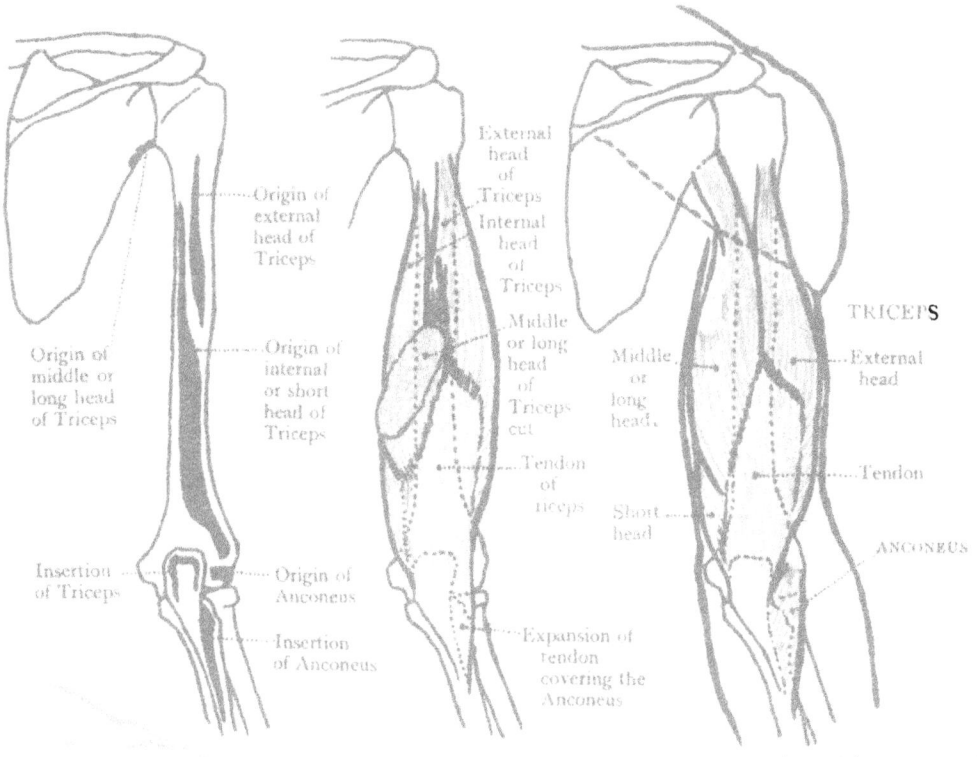

Origin of
external
head of
Triceps

External
head
of
Triceps

Internal
head
of
Triceps

Middle
or long
head
of
Triceps

TRICEPS

Origin of
middle or
long head
of Triceps

Origin of
internal
or short
head of
Triceps

Middle
or
long
head.

External
head

Middle
or long
head
of
Triceps
cut

Tendon
of
triceps

Short
head

Tendon

ANCONEUS

Insertion
of Triceps

Origin of
Anconeus

Insertion
of Anconeus

Expansion of
tendon
covering the
Anconeus

Deltoid
prominence

Teres major

Furrow of
outer head
of Triceps

Plane of
Triceps
tendon

Groove
between
olecranon
and inner condyle

Inner condyle
of Humerus

Depression
at outer
condyle

Long
radial
extensor
of the
wrist

Olecranon
process of
Ulna

Anconeus

Flexor mass
of forearm

Ulna
furrow

Diagram of the surface forms
on the back of the arm

The TRICEPS muscle, situated on the back of the arm, extends the entire length of the back of the Humerus. It is divided above into three parts, named :

1. The middle, or long head,
2. The external head,
3. The internal, or short head.

The middle or long head arises from a depression immediately below the glenoid cavity of the Scapula. The external head arises from the upper and outer part of the back of the Humerus. The internal head arises from the back of the Humerus and from its inner border, commencing above narrow and pointed and extending below near to the trochlear surface. The *common tendon* of the Triceps receives the muscular fibres from the three heads ; it commences about the middle of the back of the muscle and causes a very important flattened surface form. It is inserted below into the olecranon process of the Ulna, an expansion of the tendon being continued downwards on the outer side, passing over the Anconeus muscle, to blend with the deep fascia of the forearm. The long head of the Triceps passes between the Teres minor and Teres major muscles.

The ANCONEUS muscle is a small triangular muscle, placed behind and below the elbow joint. It appears to be a continuation of the outer portion of the Triceps. It arises from the back of the outer condyle of the Humerus, and is inserted into the side of the olecranon process and the upper fourth of the back of the shaft of the Ulna

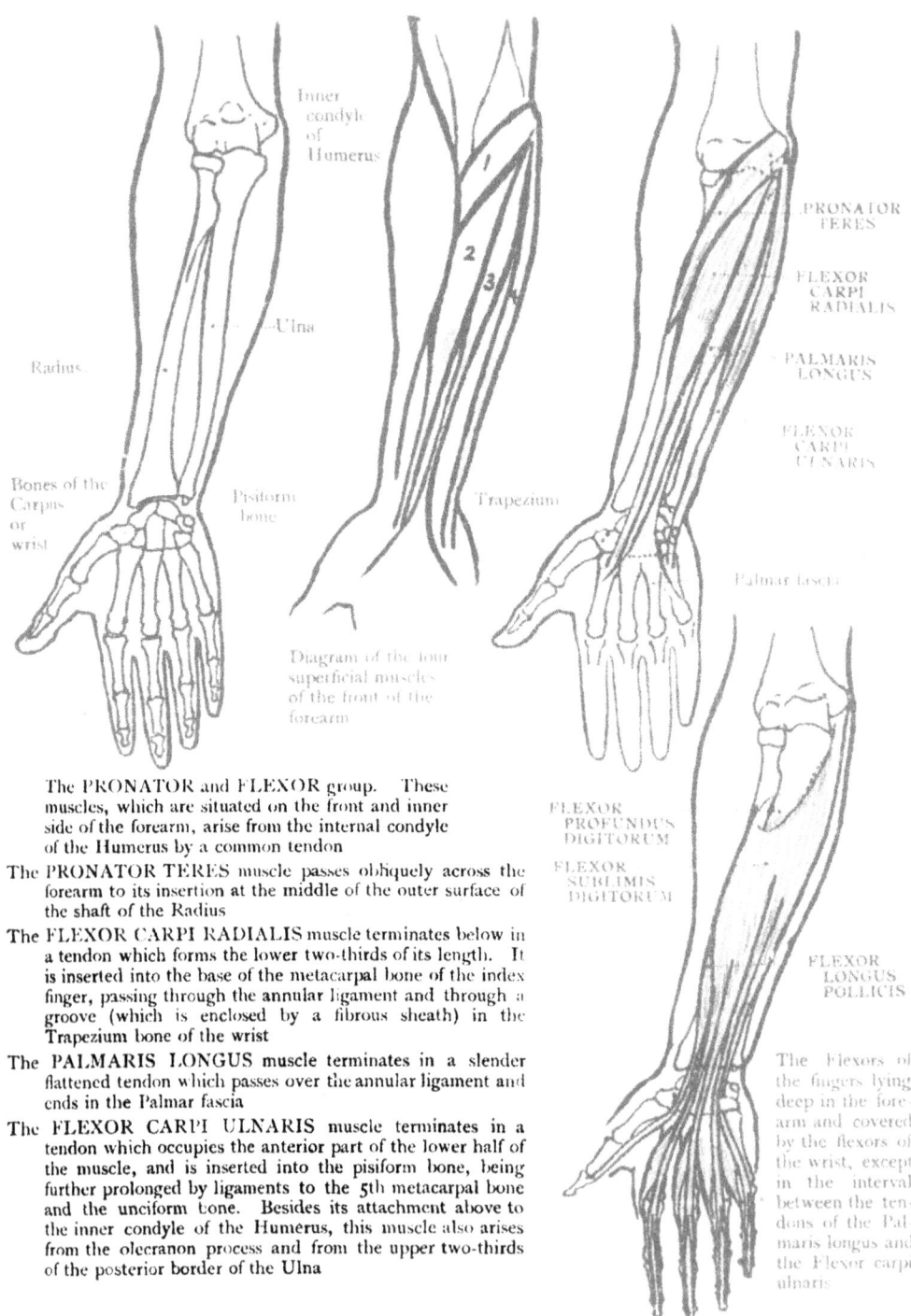

Inner condyle of Humerus

Ulna

Radius

Bones of the Carpus or wrist

Pisiform bone

Trapezium

Diagram of the four superficial muscles of the front of the forearm

PRONATOR TERES

FLEXOR CARPI RADIALIS

PALMARIS LONGUS

FLEXOR CARPI ULNARIS

Palmar fascia

FLEXOR PROFUNDUS DIGITORUM

FLEXOR SUBLIMIS DIGITORUM

FLEXOR LONGUS POLLICIS

The PRONATOR and FLEXOR group. These muscles, which are situated on the front and inner side of the forearm, arise from the internal condyle of the Humerus by a common tendon

The PRONATOR TERES muscle passes obliquely across the forearm to its insertion at the middle of the outer surface of the shaft of the Radius

The FLEXOR CARPI RADIALIS muscle terminates below in a tendon which forms the lower two-thirds of its length. It is inserted into the base of the metacarpal bone of the index finger, passing through the annular ligament and through a groove (which is enclosed by a fibrous sheath) in the Trapezium bone of the wrist

The PALMARIS LONGUS muscle terminates in a slender flattened tendon which passes over the annular ligament and ends in the Palmar fascia

The FLEXOR CARPI ULNARIS muscle terminates in a tendon which occupies the anterior part of the lower half of the muscle, and is inserted into the pisiform bone, being further prolonged by ligaments to the 5th metacarpal bone and the unciform bone. Besides its attachment above to the inner condyle of the Humerus, this muscle also arises from the olecranon process and from the upper two-thirds of the posterior border of the Ulna

The Flexors of the fingers lying deep in the forearm and covered by the flexors of the wrist, except in the interval between the tendons of the Palmaris longus and the Flexor carpi ulnaris

# MUSCLES OF BACK AND OUTER SIDE OF FOREARM.

## THE SUPINATOR AND EXTENSOR GROUP.

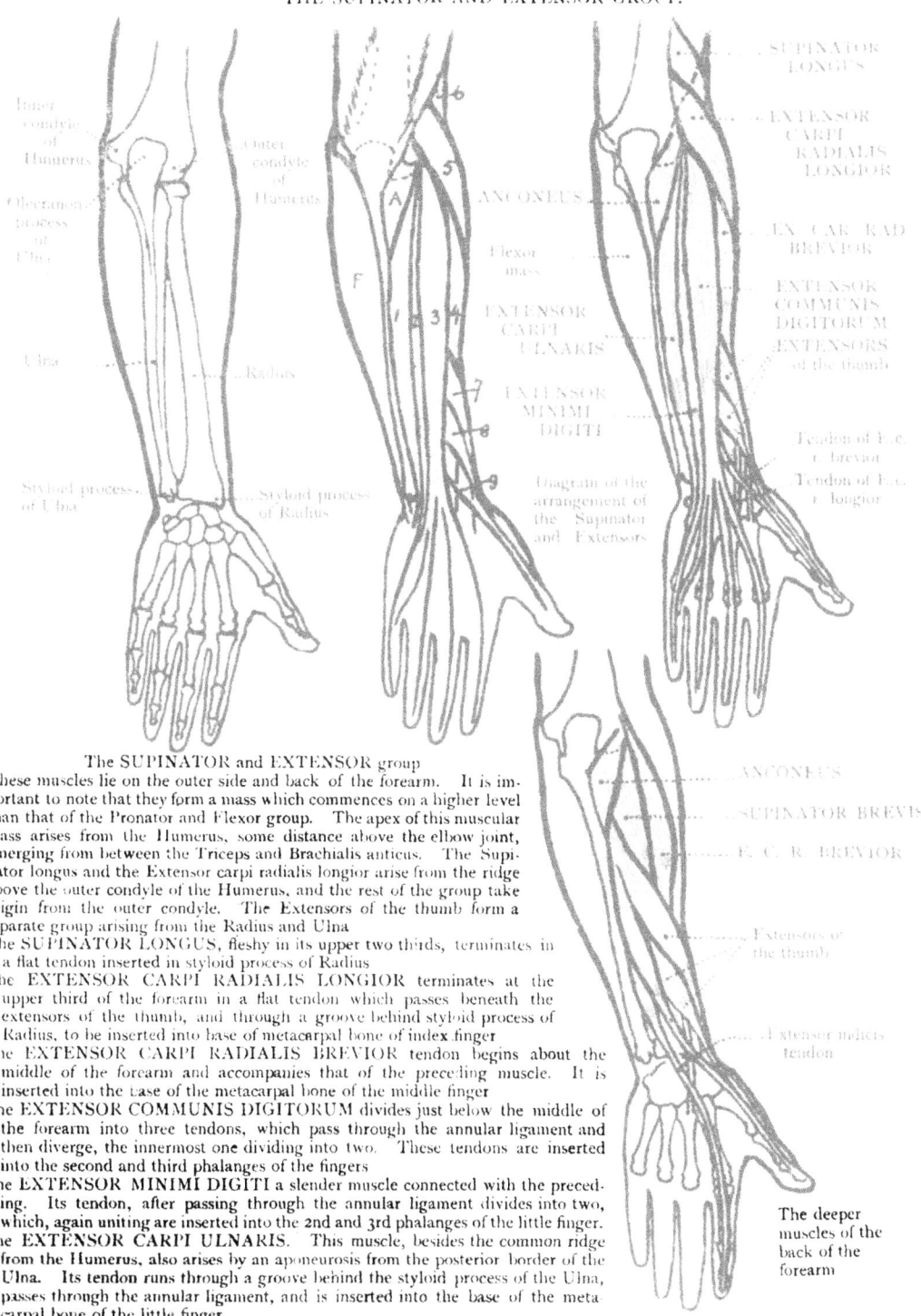

Inner condyle of Humerus

Olecranon process of Ulna

Ulna

Radius

Styloid process of Ulna

Outer condyle of Humerus

Styloid process of Radius

ANCONEUS

Flexor mass

EXTENSOR CARPI ULNARIS

EXTENSOR MINIMI DIGITI

Diagram of the arrangement of the Supinator and Extensors

SUPINATOR LONGUS

EXTENSOR CARPI RADIALIS LONGIOR

EX. CAR. RAD. BREVIOR

EXTENSOR COMMUNIS DIGITORUM

EXTENSORS of the thumb

Tendon of E. c. r brevior

Tendon of E. c. r longior

ANCONEUS

SUPINATOR BREVIS

E. C. R. BREVIOR

Extensors of the thumb

Extensor indicis tendon

The deeper muscles of the back of the forearm

The SUPINATOR and EXTENSOR group

These muscles lie on the outer side and back of the forearm. It is important to note that they form a mass which commences on a higher level than that of the Pronator and Flexor group. The apex of this muscular mass arises from the Humerus, some distance above the elbow joint, emerging from between the Triceps and Brachialis anticus. The Supinator longus and the Extensor carpi radialis longior arise from the ridge above the outer condyle of the Humerus, and the rest of the group take origin from the outer condyle. The Extensors of the thumb form a separate group arising from the Radius and Ulna

The SUPINATOR LONGUS, fleshy in its upper two thirds, terminates in a flat tendon inserted in styloid process of Radius

The EXTENSOR CARPI RADIALIS LONGIOR terminates at the upper third of the forearm in a flat tendon which passes beneath the extensors of the thumb, and through a groove behind styloid process of Radius, to be inserted into base of metacarpal bone of index finger

The EXTENSOR CARPI RADIALIS BREVIOR tendon begins about the middle of the forearm and accompanies that of the preceding muscle. It is inserted into the base of the metacarpal bone of the middle finger

The EXTENSOR COMMUNIS DIGITORUM divides just below the middle of the forearm into three tendons, which pass through the annular ligament and then diverge, the innermost one dividing into two. These tendons are inserted into the second and third phalanges of the fingers

The EXTENSOR MINIMI DIGITI a slender muscle connected with the preceding. Its tendon, after passing through the annular ligament divides into two, which, again uniting are inserted into the 2nd and 3rd phalanges of the little finger.

The EXTENSOR CARPI ULNARIS. This muscle, besides the common ridge from the Humerus, also arises by an aponeurosis from the posterior border of the Ulna. Its tendon runs through a groove behind the styloid process of the Ulna, passes through the annular ligament, and is inserted into the base of the metacarpal bone of the little finger

61

# BONES OF THE HAND.—PALMAR VIEW.

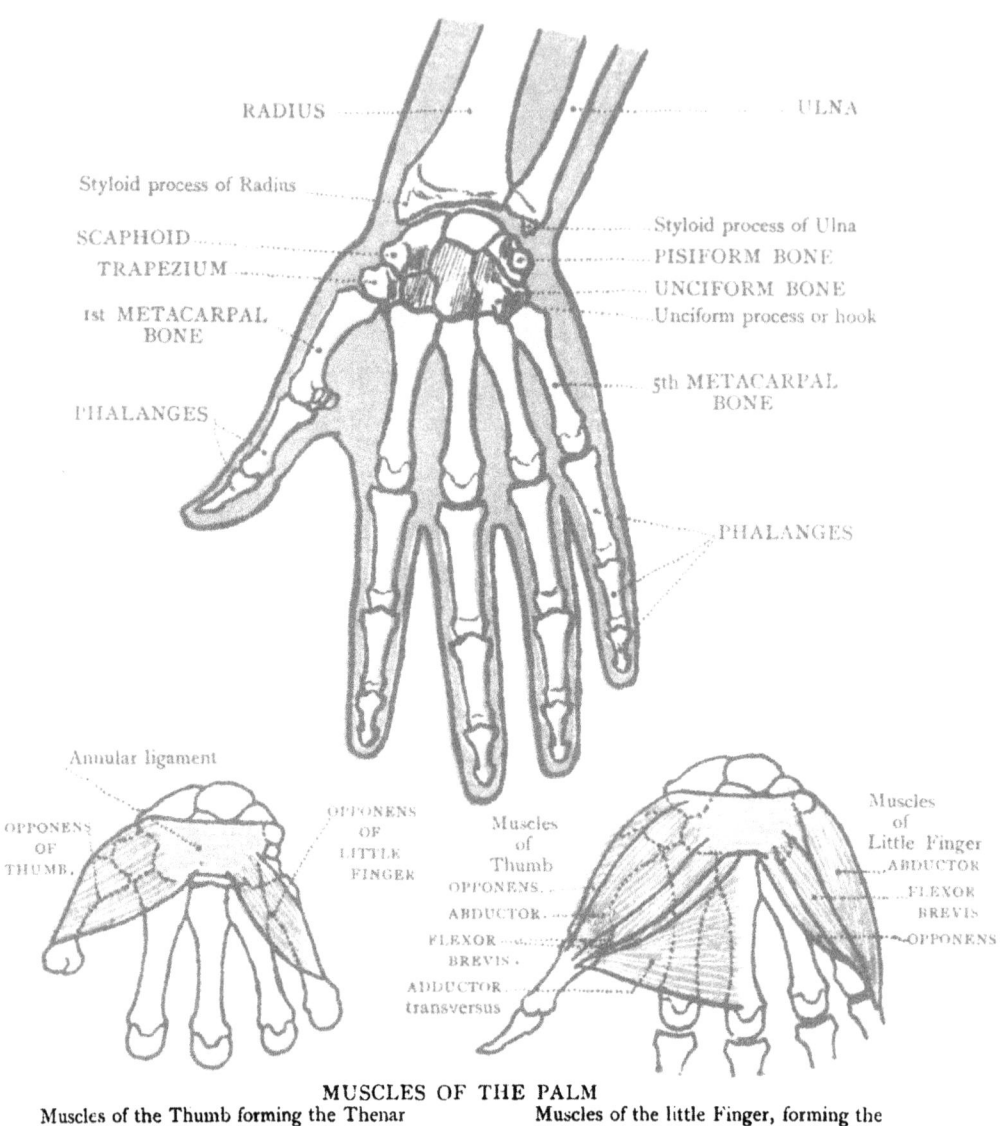

RADIUS

ULNA

Styloid process of Radius

SCAPHOID

TRAPEZIUM

1st METACARPAL BONE

PHALANGES

Styloid process of Ulna

PISIFORM BONE

UNCIFORM BONE

Unciform process or hook

5th METACARPAL BONE

PHALANGES

Annular ligament

OPPONENS OF THUMB

OPPONENS OF LITTLE FINGER

Muscles of Thumb

OPPONENS

ABDUCTOR

FLEXOR BREVIS

ADDUCTOR transversus

Muscles of Little Finger

ABDUCTOR

FLEXOR BREVIS

OPPONENS

## MUSCLES OF THE PALM

Muscles of the Thumb forming the Thenar eminence or ball of the thumb

1. OPPONENS POLLICIS
2. FLEXOR BREVIS POLLICIS
3. ABDUCTOR POLLICIS
4. ADDUCTOR } transversus and
   POLLICIS } obliquus

Muscles of the little Finger, forming the Hypothenar eminence or ball of little finger

1. ABDUCTOR MINIMI DIGITI
2. FLEXOR BREVIS ,, ,,
3. OPPONENS ,, ,,

| | Origin | Insertion |
|---|---|---|
| The ABDUCTOR MINIMI DIGITI ... | From the Pisiform bone | ... 1st phalanx of little finger |
| The FLEXOR BREVIS ,, ,, ... | from unciform process of unciform bone and from | ... do. do. |
| The OPPONENS ,, ,, ... | the annular ligament | ... Metacarpal bone |

In the middle of the Palm are the Lumbricales, four small muscles, accessories to the deep Flexor of the fingers; and in the intervals between the metacarpal bones, are the Interossci muscles, 4 dorsal and 3 palmar

# MUSCLES OF THE HAND.—PALMAR VIEW.

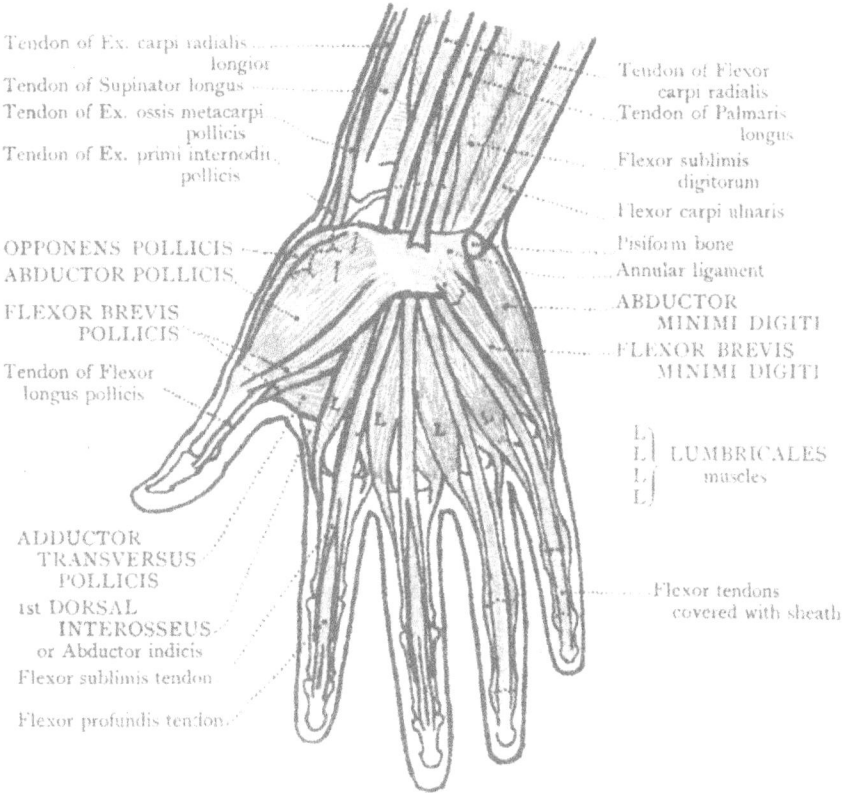

Tendon of Ex. carpi radialis
    longior
Tendon of Supinator longus
Tendon of Ex. ossis metacarpi
    pollicis
Tendon of Ex. primi internodii
    pollicis

OPPONENS POLLICIS
ABDUCTOR POLLICIS

FLEXOR BREVIS
    POLLICIS

Tendon of Flexor
    longus pollicis

ADDUCTOR
   TRANSVERSUS
    POLLICIS
1st DORSAL
   INTEROSSEUS
   or Abductor indicis
Flexor sublimis tendon

Flexor profundis tendon

Tendon of Flexor
   carpi radialis
Tendon of Palmaris
   longus
Flexor sublimis
   digitorum
Flexor carpi ulnaris
Pisiform bone
Annular ligament
ABDUCTOR
   MINIMI DIGITI
FLEXOR BREVIS
   MINIMI DIGITI

L
L
L  LUMBRICALES
L   muscles
L

Flexor tendons
   covered with sheath

The THUMB is provided with the following muscles :—
3 Extensors situated on the back of the forearm and hand ;
3 Flexors, 1 Abductor and 2 Adductors, all muscles of the palm, except the Flexor Longus, which has its fleshy part deep in the front of the forearm

EXTENSORS
   EX. OSSIS METACARPI POLLICIS inserted into the......Metacarpal bone
   ,, PRIMI INTERNODII POLLICIS   ..   .,  .........1st Phalanx
   ,, SECUNDI INTERNODII POLLICIS .,   ..  ........terminal Phalanx
FLEXORS
   OPPONENS POLLICIS arises from the Trapezium and
     annular ligament and is inserted into the........................ Metacarpal bone
   FLEXOR BREVIS POLLICIS consists of two portions :
     the outer arises from the Trapezium and annular
     ligament and is inserted into the.............................1st Phalanx, outer side
     The inner and deeper portion arises from the meta-
     carpal bone of the thumb and is inserted along with
     the Adductor obliquus into the.............................1st Phalanx, inner side
     A sesamoid bone is developed in each of the two
     tendons of insertion
   FLEXOR LONGUS POLLICIS, a deep muscle of the
     forearm having an extensive origin from the Radius ;
     it is inserted into the ...................................................terminal Phalanx
ABDUCTOR and ADDUCTORS
   ABDUCTOR POLLICIS arises from Trapezium and
     annular ligament and is inserted into the ..................... 1st Phalanx
   ADDUCTOR   ⎫ obliquus, from the Os magnum, etc.,
   POLLICIS    ⎬ transversus, from the metacarpal bone   inserted into
           ⎭ of the middle finger... ...........................1st Phalanx.

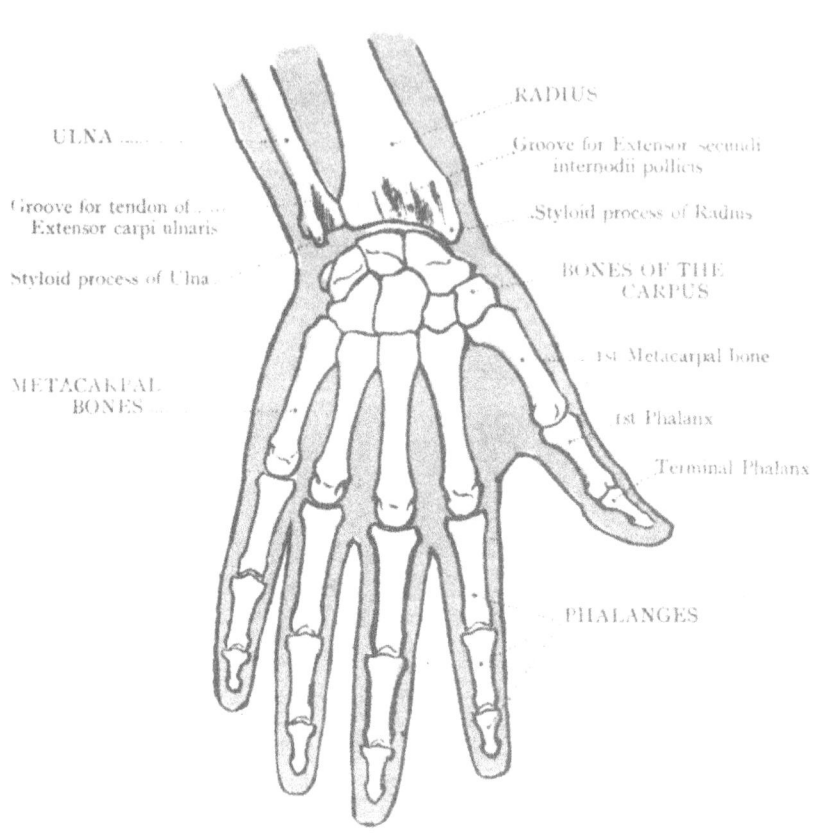

RADIUS

ULNA

Groove for Extensor secundi
internodii pollicis

Groove for tendon of
Extensor carpi ulnaris

Styloid process of Radius

Styloid process of Ulna

BONES OF THE
CARPUS

1st Metacarpal bone

METACARPAL
BONES

1st Phalanx

Terminal Phalanx

PHALANGES

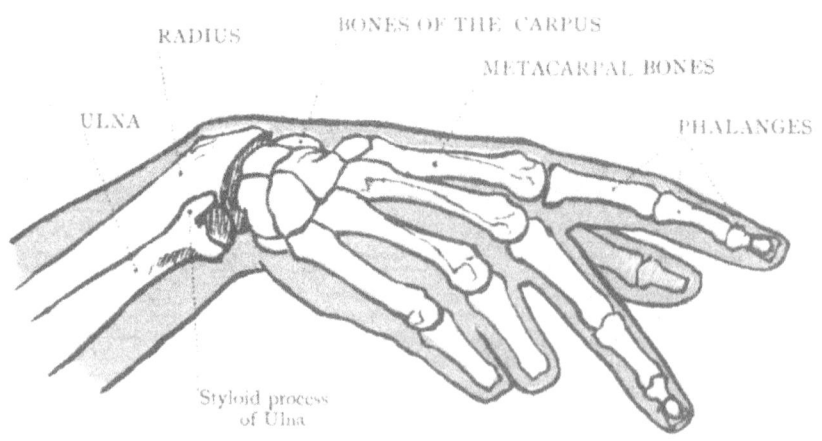

RADIUS

BONES OF THE CARPUS

METACARPAL BONES

ULNA

PHALANGES

Styloid process
of Ulna

# MUSCLES OF THE HAND.—BACK VIEW.

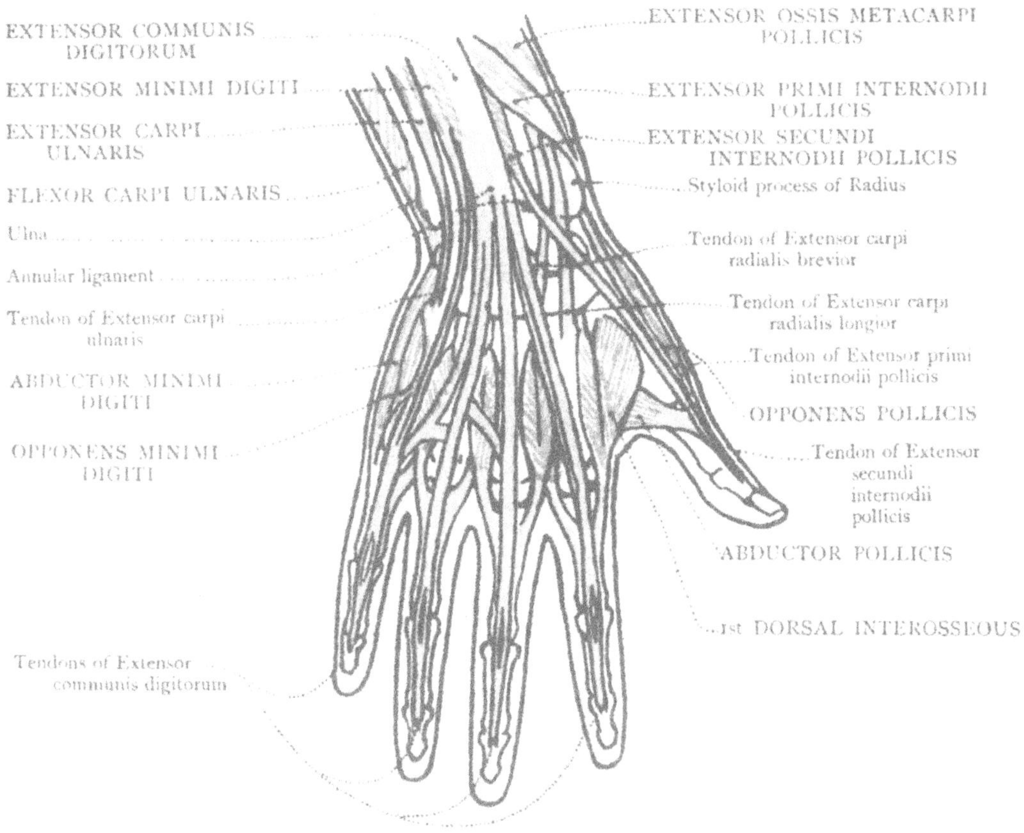

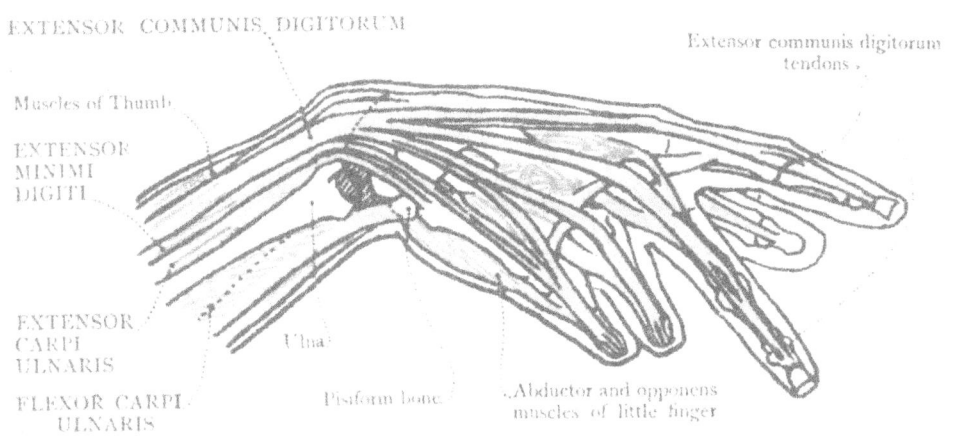

EXTENSOR COMMUNIS DIGITORUM

EXTENSOR MINIMI DIGITI

EXTENSOR CARPI ULNARIS

FLEXOR CARPI ULNARIS

Ulna

Annular ligament

Tendon of Extensor carpi ulnaris

ABDUCTOR MINIMI DIGITI

OPPONENS MINIMI DIGITI

Tendons of Extensor communis digitorum

EXTENSOR OSSIS METACARPI POLLICIS

EXTENSOR PRIMI INTERNODII POLLICIS

EXTENSOR SECUNDI INTERNODII POLLICIS

Styloid process of Radius

Tendon of Extensor carpi radialis brevior

Tendon of Extensor carpi radialis longior

Tendon of Extensor primi internodii pollicis

OPPONENS POLLICIS

Tendon of Extensor secundi internodii pollicis

ABDUCTOR POLLICIS

1st DORSAL INTEROSSEOUS

EXTENSOR COMMUNIS DIGITORUM

Muscles of Thumb

EXTENSOR MINIMI DIGITI

EXTENSOR CARPI ULNARIS

FLEXOR CARPI ULNARIS

Ulna

Pisiform bone

Extensor communis digitorum tendons

Abductor and opponens muscles of little finger

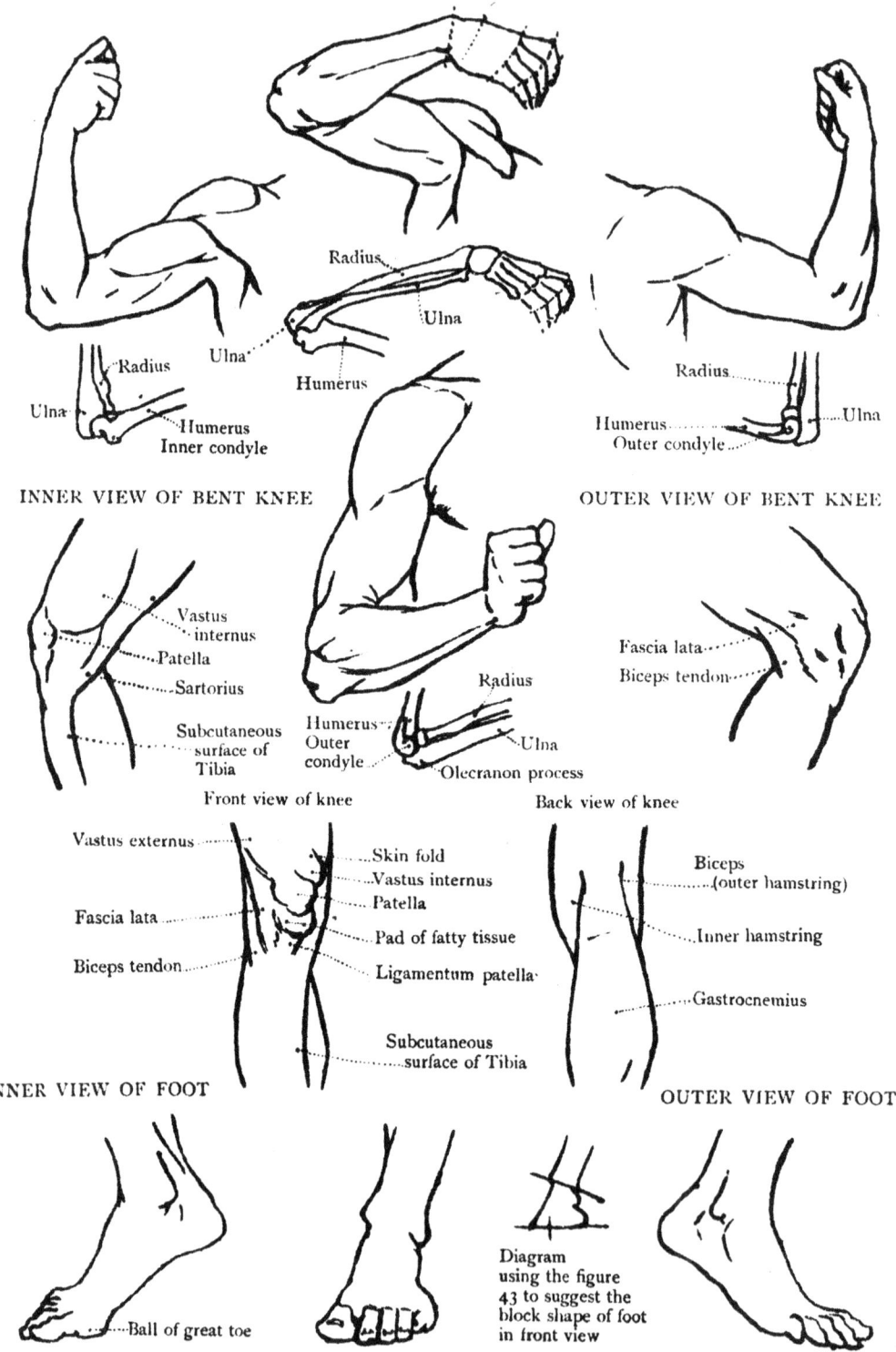

Radius

Ulna

Radius

Ulna

Humerus

Ulna

Radius

Ulna

Humerus
Inner condyle

Radius

Humerus........Ulna
Outer condyle

INNER VIEW OF BENT KNEE

OUTER VIEW OF BENT KNEE

Vastus
internus
Patella
Sartorius

Subcutaneous
surface of
Tibia

Fascia lata
Biceps tendon

Humerus
Outer
condyle

Radius

Ulna

Olecranon process

Front view of knee

Back view of knee

Vastus externus

Skin fold
Vastus internus
Patella

Biceps
(outer hamstring)

Fascia lata

Inner hamstring

Biceps tendon

Pad of fatty tissue

Ligamentum patella

Gastrocnemius

Subcutaneous
surface of Tibia

INNER VIEW OF FOOT

OUTER VIEW OF FOOT

Ball of great toe

Diagram
using the figure
43 to suggest the
block shape of foot
in front view

# BONES OF THE UPPER AND LOWER LIMBS.

Bones of the
UPPER LIMB,
front view, with the forearm
in the position of
PRONATION

NOTE.—The illustrations on
this page, and also those of
the skeleton of the trunk in
three-quarter front and back
views, are from photographs
of artificially articulated
bones

Bones of the
LOWER LIMB
in bent position
Outer view

Bones of the
UPPER LIMB,
front view, with the
forearm in the posi-
tion of
SUPINATION

NOTE.—The bones of
the upper limb are
here shown on a
larger scale than those
of the lower limb

Bones of the
LOWER LIMB
in bent position
Front view

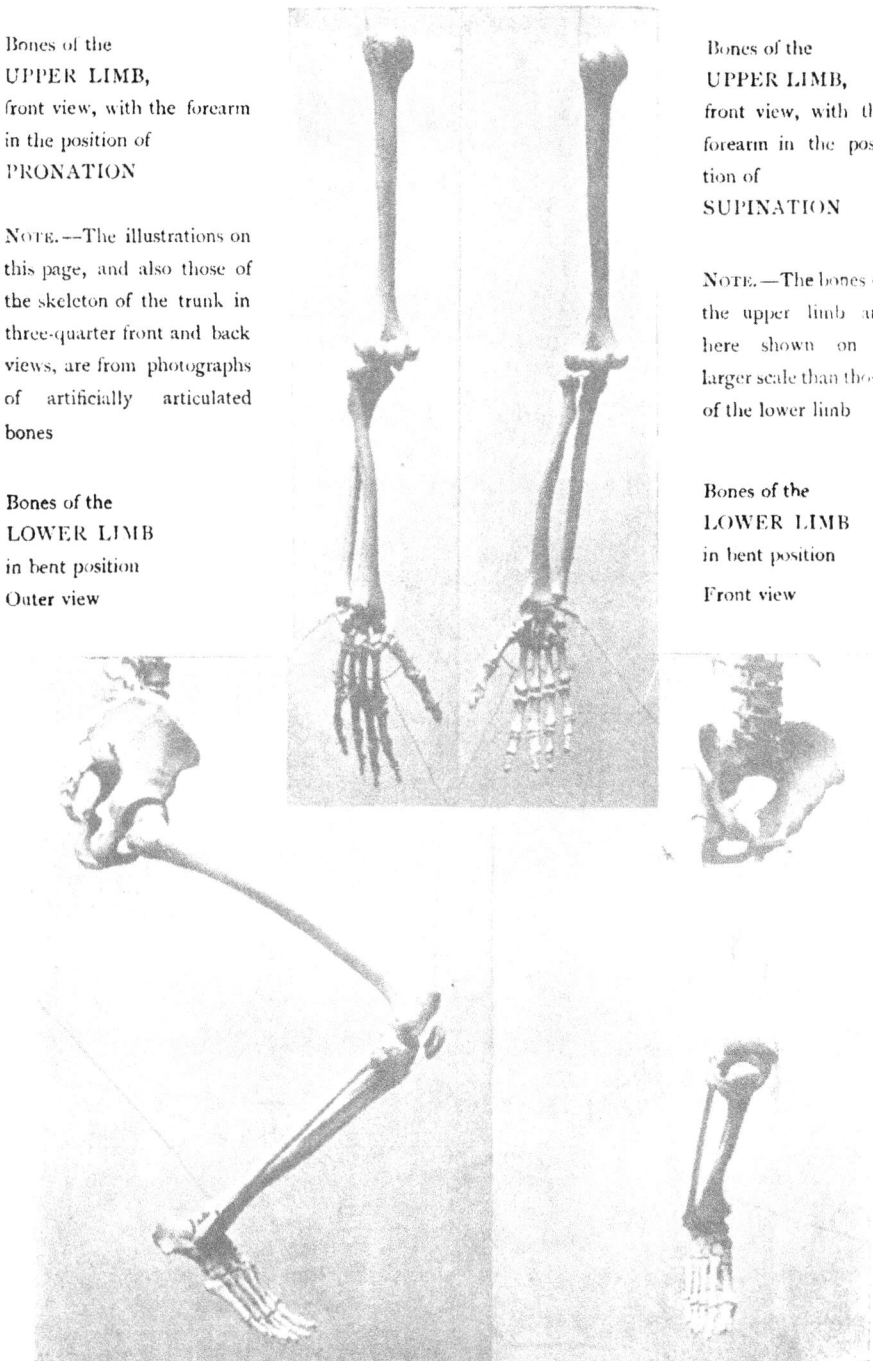

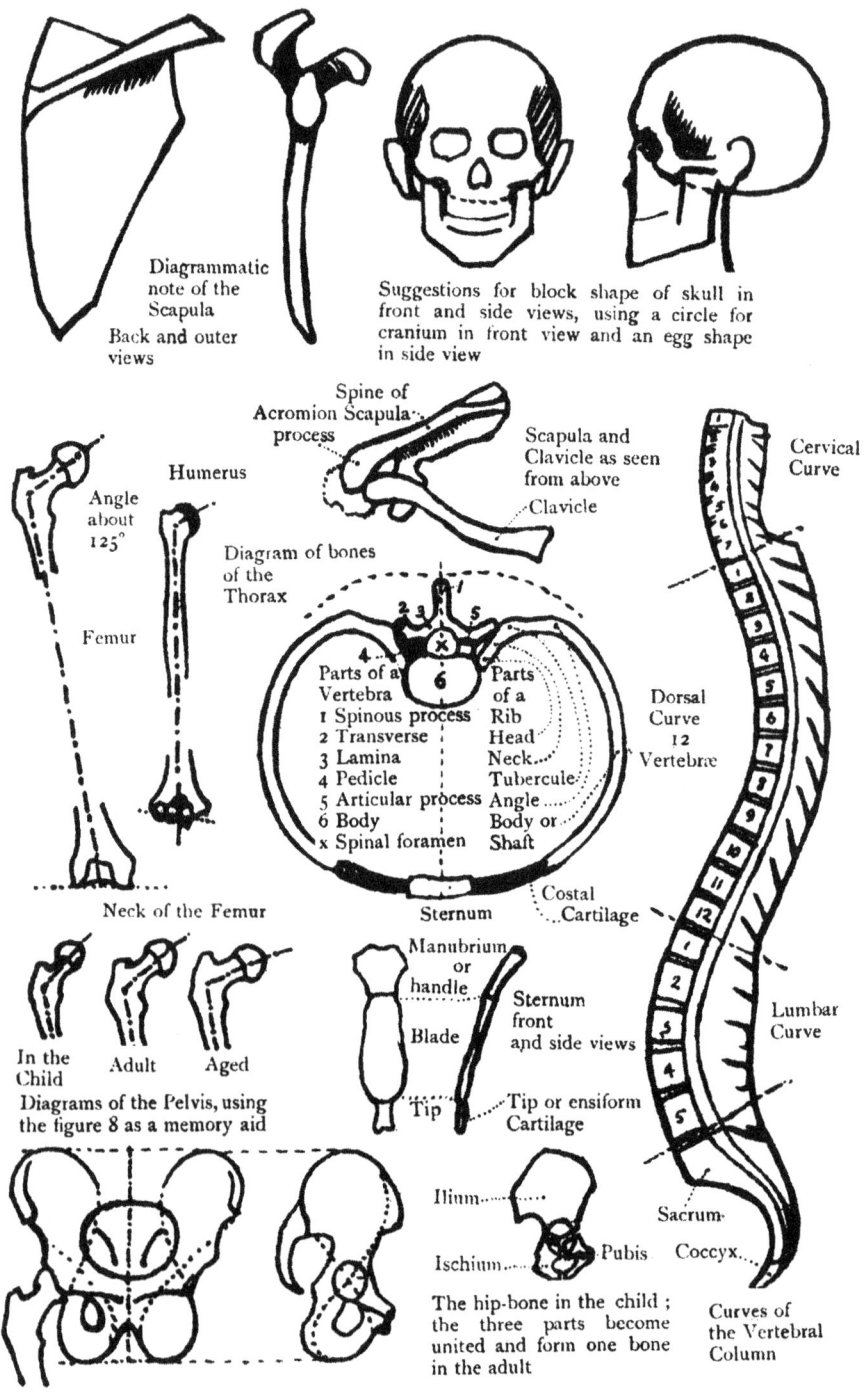

Diagrammatic note of the Scapula
Back and outer views

Suggestions for block shape of skull in front and side views, using a circle for cranium in front view and an egg shape in side view

Spine of Scapula

Acromion process

Scapula and Clavicle as seen from above

Clavicle

Cervical Curve

Humerus

Angle about 125°

Diagram of bones of the Thorax

Femur

Parts of a Vertebra
1 Spinous process
2 Transverse
3 Lamina
4 Pedicle
5 Articular process
6 Body
x Spinal foramen

Parts of a Rib
Head
Neck
Tubercle
Angle
Body or Shaft

Dorsal Curve
12 Vertebræ

Neck of the Femur

Sternum

Costal Cartilage

In the Child      Adult      Aged

Diagrams of the Pelvis, using the figure 8 as a memory aid

Manubrium or handle

Blade

Sternum front and side views

Tip

Tip or ensiform Cartilage

Lumbar Curve

Sacrum

Ilium

Ischium

Pubis

Coccyx

The hip-bone in the child; the three parts become united and form one bone in the adult

Curves of the Vertebral Column

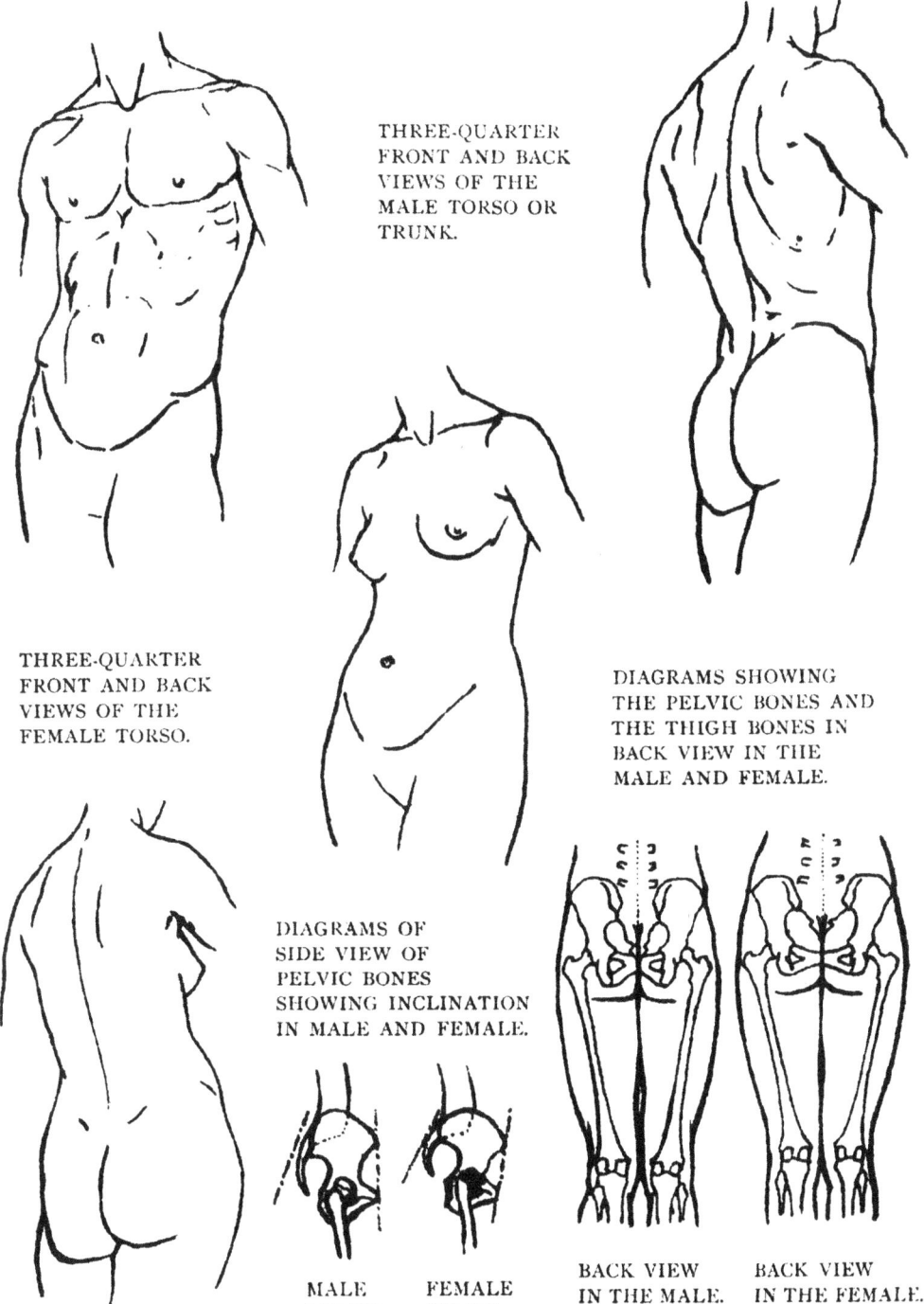

THREE-QUARTER
FRONT AND BACK
VIEWS OF THE
MALE TORSO OR
TRUNK.

THREE-QUARTER
FRONT AND BACK
VIEWS OF THE
FEMALE TORSO.

DIAGRAMS SHOWING
THE PELVIC BONES AND
THE THIGH BONES IN
BACK VIEW IN THE
MALE AND FEMALE.

DIAGRAMS OF
SIDE VIEW OF
PELVIC BONES
SHOWING INCLINATION
IN MALE AND FEMALE.

MALE
PELVIS.

FEMALE
PELVIS.

BACK VIEW
IN THE MALE.

BACK VIEW
IN THE FEMALE.

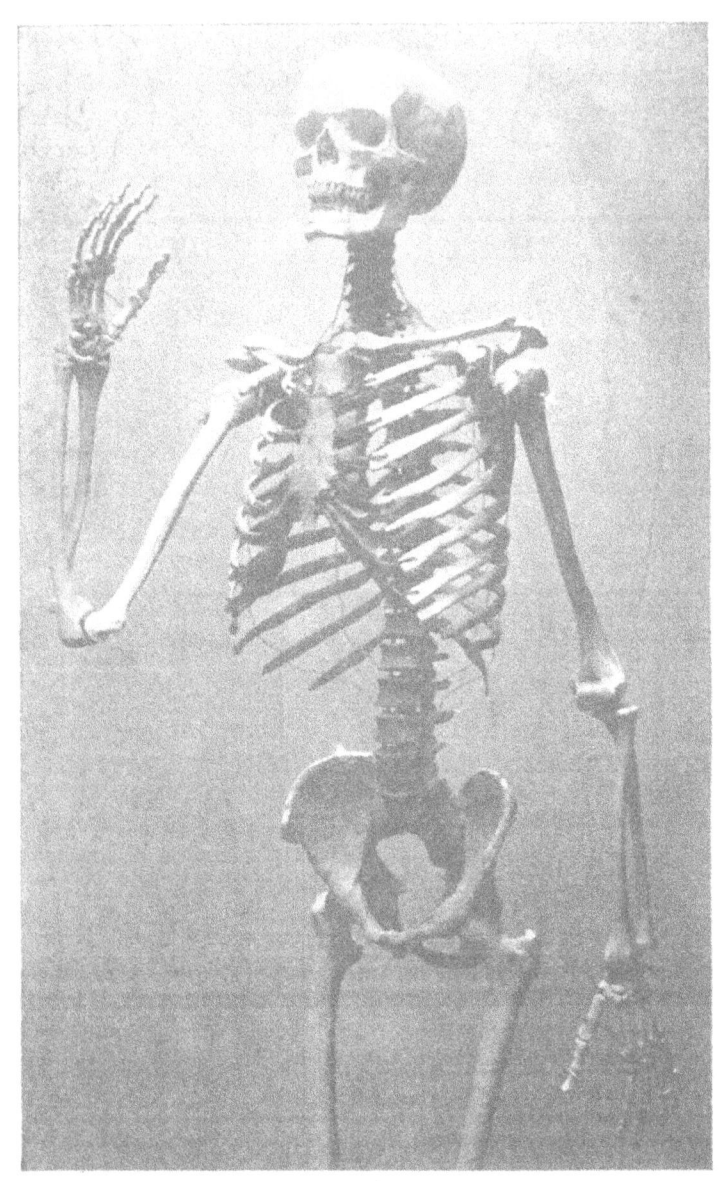

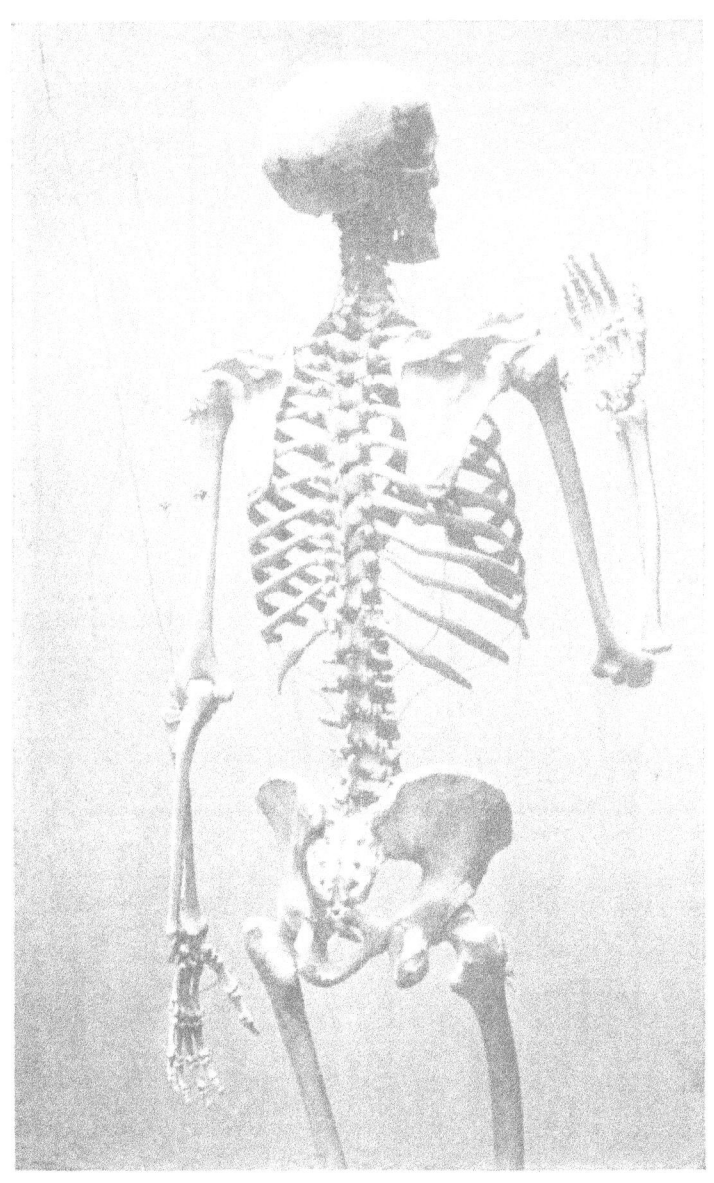

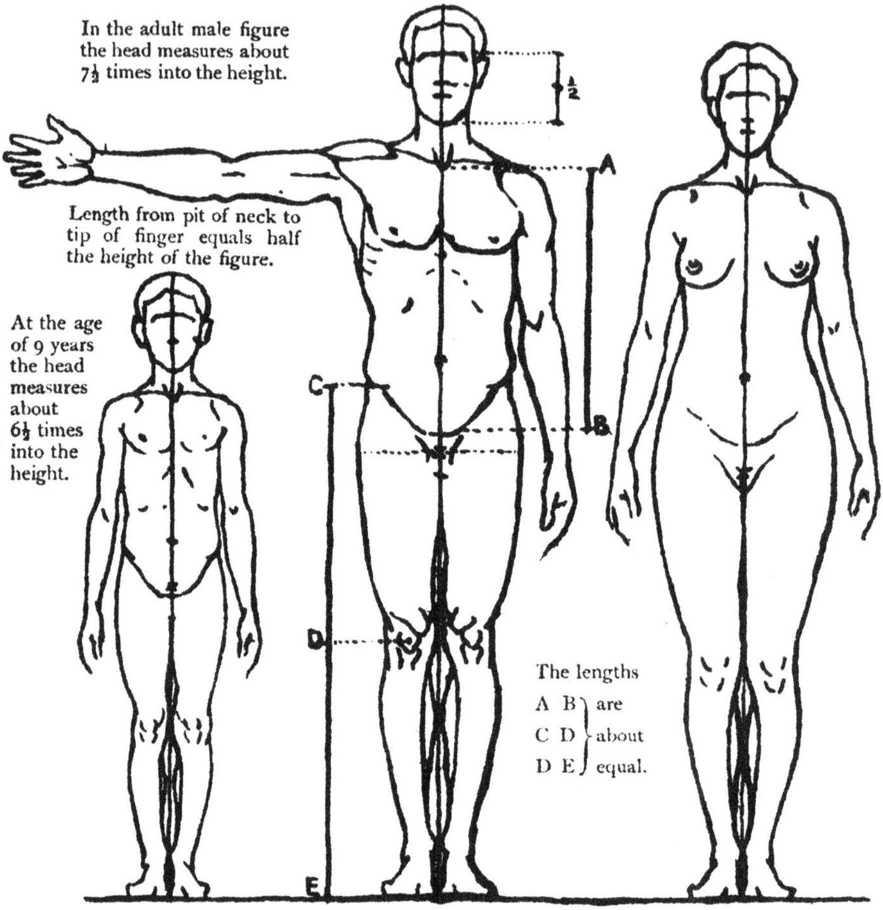

# DIAGRAMS WITH NOTES ON PROPORTION.

In the adult male figure the head measures about 7½ times into the height.

Length from pit of neck to tip of finger equals half the height of the figure.

At the age of 9 years the head measures about 6½ times into the height.

½

A

C

B

D

The lengths
A B ⎫ are
C D ⎬ about
D E ⎭ equal.

E

Relation of Head to height of figure.
At Birth.    5 years.    Adult.

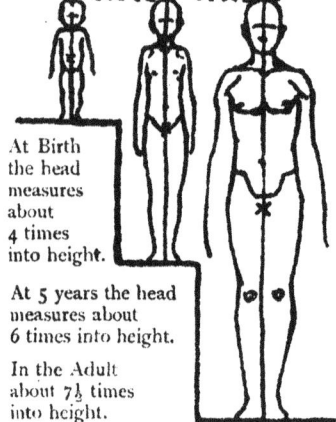

At Birth the head measures about 4 times into height.

At 5 years the head measures about 6 times into height.

In the Adult about 7½ times into height.

In the adult male figure, in the upright position, the distance from the top of the head to the pit of the neck measures about 5½ times into the height; this distance is about equal to the greatest width at the hips, or middle of the height of the figure. The greatest width at the shoulders, at the fullest point of the deltoid muscle, is about equal to 2 heads, or more than one quarter of the height.

In the female figure, the distance from the top of the head to the waist is about ½ of the height. The width at the shoulders is slightly less proportionately than in the male figure, but the width at the hips is proportionately, or even absolutely, greater in the female, and is at a lower level, being a little below the great trochanters. The width at the hips measures about 4⅔ times into the height, and is about equal to the distance from the pit of the neck to the umbilicus.

72